SCENT OF HEAVEN
For we are unto God a sweet fragrance of Christ,
in them that are saved, and in them that perish:
(2 Corinthians 2:17)

SCENT of HEAVEN

For we are unto God a sweet fragrance of Christ,
In them that are saved, and in them that perish:
(2 Corinthians 2:17)

Prayer and Daily Spiritual Insight

Synetra Evette Leaphart

XULON PRESS

Xulon Press
2301 Lucien Way #415
Maitland, FL 32751
407.339.4217
www.xulonpress.com

© 2018 by Synetra Evette Leaphart

All rights reserved solely by the author. The author guarantees all contents are original and do not infringe upon the legal rights of any other person or work. No part of this book may be reproduced in any form without the permission of the author. The views expressed in this book are not necessarily those of the publisher.

Unless otherwise indicated, Scripture quotations taken from the King James Version (KJV)–*public domain*.

Edited by Xulon Press.

Printed in the United States of America.

ISBN-13: 978-1-54563-477-6

FOREWORD

It is my distinct pleasure and honor to take this opportunity to congratulate my wife, soul-mate and love of my life, on completing her first book. I say first book because I know there are many more to follow. It is a really great inspirational book that I know will bless every reader. It is an easy read that will connect you with God, as well as reach a level in your spiritual growth where you're thirsty for more. I declare and decree this book will be life transforming and be a number 1 best seller, in Jesus' name. It is my prayer to God for all readers to receive as special blessing as they read the messages each day.

Peace and Grace
Bishop Richard Leaphart-Mack

PREFACE

Peace and blessings to you all... I thank God for my husband, Richard A. Mack-Leaphart, who afforded me this great opportunity to share my spiritual journey with you. This inspirational book is based on my personal journey with the Lord, during my valley experiences. It is intended to connect the readers to God on a more deeper level, including Him in your everyday ventures. We, as Christians, can not do anything without spending time communing with God. Understanding, He is always there, listening, waiting to hear our voice. It's a sweet smelling Savior to Him, He loves it when we communicate with Him, as well as invoking His very presence into our every day lives. It is my sincere prayer that you walk away everyday with a deeper and closer relationship with our God. He loves us! May God richly bless the readers of this daily inspirational book.

JANUARY

Revelation 21:5 KJV - And he that sat upon the throne said, Behold, I make all things new. And he said unto me, Write: for these words are true and faithful.

JANUARY 1

Prayer: Lord, I trust you. Those were the four words you gave me over twelve years ago, and those are the words that I will forever cling to. I have no better choice; you are my ultimate source, and my life is already in you, so whom shall I fear or be afraid of. You have kept me in perfect peace. Though storms come, they also go. I must trust that the storm is under your total control, and you will do nothing to harm my soul. Though the flesh may suffer, you will keep me—as long as I keep my eyes on you and trust the process of the journey that you have established for me I know that in the end, I win over each storm. With you all things are possible. Lord, I will forever trust you and stack my treasures in Heaven, retrieving them as I need to. You are my source. I love you, in Jesus' name.

Psalm 56:3-4 (KJV)
> What time I am afraid, I will trust in thee. [4] In God I will praise his word, in God I have put my trust; I will not fear what flesh can do unto me.

Matthew 6:20-21 (KJV)
> But lay up for yourselves treasures in heaven, where neither moth nor rust doth corrupt, and where thieves do not break through nor steal: [21] For where your treasure is, there will your heart be also.

January 2

Today is a beautiful day, filled with wonders and amazement of your miraculous working power in nature. His is truly your world, and I will be obedient in not cursing your creation by speaking negatively. It's not the world that is corrupt but those who dwell in your beautiful creation. I will make known my request to you and with supplication and thanksgiving wait for the manifestation of your promise to come to pass. I trust all of your promises to take care of me and all that relates to my total being. I relinquish to you the power I thought I had. I give you total control and will not take it back from you. I trust that you have it all in control. Without you, I would mess up every time.

Prayer: Most righteous, loving, and great God, I give back to you what is already yours—me. Take all of me; use me for your Kingdom service. Without you, I can do nothing, I can be nothing aside from you. I thank you for understanding wisdom and your Holy Spirit who dwells inside of me and is my keeper and guide. You are my wonderful counselor, in you, God and you only, I live move and have my being.

Psalm 46:10 (KJV)
> Be still, and know that I am God: I will be exalted among the heathen, I will be exalted in the earth.

JANUARY 3

Prayer: Lord I thank you for giving me your grace and peace. I come to you openly, not hiding my emptiness, shortcomings, brokenness, loneliness, or even regrets. All of these are feelings that my soul reacts to due to things I've suffered. I can't handle them, so I cast them at your feet. I release all negativity that is burdensome to my soul. You know my ending from the beginning and all that I would encounter whether good or bad; you even know my thoughts before they are uttered from my lips. You know me better than I'll ever know myself, yet you love me in all my frailties and disappointments. I trust you, Lord, with my heart and mind. Continue to transform me so that I am like you. Righteousness is what I desire from you. I give myself to you. Use me as an instrument of praise and worship, reaching the lost, teaching, and being an example to them of what righteousness is all about. All things are naked before you. I have no need of pretense because a liar cannot tarry in your sight. In this, I'm persuaded that life challenges, no matter what they are, shall not separate me from you. We are together forever. Thank you, Lord, for choosing such an unworthy being to serve in your Kingdom.

Romans 8:38–39 (KJV)
> For I am persuaded, that neither death, nor life, nor angels, nor principalities, nor powers, nor things present, nor things to come, [39] Nor height, nor depth, nor any other creature, shall be able to separate us from the love of God, which is in Christ Jesus our Lord.

January 4

Prayer: You did it all for me, Lord, all just for me, whom you knew needed you, my Savior. You suffered, bled, and died a shameful death so that I might live a life of peace though the storms of life rage. You did it so that I might live a life of abundance though there's recession throughout the world and that I might possess great power though my body might be frail and weak. You did it so that I would inherit eternal life with you. Though my limited mind is unable to comprehend the limitless possibilities I have in you, through the Spirit, I know I can do all things through you and the power of Holy Spirit. I will not fear man who can only destroy this physical body that houses my spirit man. You are the only one I fear. I have fixed my heart and my eyes on you. I stand fast in my holy armor, and I hold fast to your holy word. I am more than a conqueror in and through you. Use me for your service for such a time as this.

Hebrews 12:2 (KJV)
> Looking unto Jesus the author and finisher of our faith; who for the joy that was set before him endured the cross, despising the shame, and is set down at the right hand of the throne of God.

January 5

Prayer: My hope and confidence is in you, Lord. I will not worry about the struggles that will come my way today or the many challenges to come. I know that you are with me, just as you were with my forefathers. I'm never alone because you are always with me. I can face tomorrow and each day thereafter with the confidence, knowing that in you I have peace. I trust you in all that I do. Your Holy Spirit shall forever guide me into all truth and protection.

Matthew 11:28-30 (KJV)
> Come unto me, all ye that labour and are heavy laden, and I will give you rest. [29] Take my yoke upon you, and learn of me; for I am meek and lowly in heart: and ye shall find rest unto your souls. [30] For my yoke is easy, and my burden is light.

January 6

Prayer: Thank you, Lord, for everything you are to me. I thank you for choosing me to be a part of your Kingdom. I am royalty because of you. I am eternally grateful and indebted to you. In you, Lord, I put total trust. I will not look to my left or my right, but I look unto you. All my help comes from you. I seek your face from morning until evening. I look to you for my needs and my wants. You are my substance and my life; you know what tomorrow will bring even though I don't. Therefore, I trust you. The peace that you have given me is beyond my understanding. You, Lord, are the very essence of the life that

I live. I will continue to make my requests known, and thank you even before it has come to pass.

Philippians 4:6-7 (KJV)
> Be careful for nothing; but in every thing by prayer and supplication with thanksgiving let your requests be made known unto God. [7] And the peace of God, which passeth all understanding, shall keep your hearts and minds through Christ Jesus.

JANUARY 7

Where God leads me, I shall follow. Though there are peaks and valleys, I will follow Him. I will not deviate from the path He has established for me, not even when it appears there is an easier pathway elsewhere. I know that the path of God will have challenges that I *must* face to help strengthen me for the heights to come. I know that things may even look bleak sometimes, but I will focus on the Lord knowing that He knows what is best for me. I can face whatever comes as long as I keep my hand in God's hand. There's no problem too big. I will reach my Canaan land with God as my guide. I can do all things with Him; without Him I would surely fail to reach the success that is before me.

Habakkuk 3:19 (KJV)
> The Lord God is my strength, and he will make my feet like hinds' feet, and he will make me to walk upon mine high places. To the chief singer on my stringed instruments.

January 8

I think about all the times I have merrily, angrily, and emptily gone through life without acknowledging or seeking your face. God, you are always there. As I rise in the morning, I will seek your face; as I go along the day, I will include you until the day ends and night falls. As I sleep, my subconscious is seeking your face. I know that I'm never alone; even when I neglect to include you, I know you are right there making my pathway smooth. I can totally count on you, even when you can't count on me. Whenever I feel a void or emptiness, I have learned to just call on your name and acknowledge you. Without fail, my day feels complete. You are my peace, and in you I put my trust, Lord. How faithful you are to me when I seek you and even when I don't.

Jeremiah 29:13 (KJV)
    And ye shall seek me, and find me, when ye shall search
    for me with all your heart.

January 9

I thank God that I'm not the boss of me and that I'm not in control of "my life," He is. I have messed up so many times and will no doubt will again, but at a minimum. I will never again trust in man or my own intellect. My God is in control of everything that concerns me, and he knows what the future holds for me. It is only to do me good and not evil. I trust that as I make plans for the day that even in the smooth days, I will give God praise and seek His counsel. I know my thoughts are not His thoughts and my ways are not His; His are far greater and perfect. He knows what will be; I don't. When the day brings twists and unexpected turns, I know God is up to something, and in the end, things will work out for my best. The Lord knows me so much better than I will ever know myself. I have no choice but to seek and trust Him in all the decisions I make. In the face of adversity, I will praise Him in advance for the expected victory that is to come.

Prayer: Each day, Lord, I dedicate to you. I will follow your lead, I will never leave you out of my day; the gift of life I will not take for granted because it is filled with your love and constant and limitless opportunities. I'm constant on your heart and mind. I know there's nothing that you will withhold from me, so even in those times that I suffer hurt, pain, disappointment, loss, and even failure, I know those are things that I must endure as you are shaping, making, and preparing me for blessings that I will appreciate. I know that the successes of this life comes from no other, only you. You, Lord, take my breath away; when I look back over life, I see how you carried me as a father carries his child when she's still tender and without strength in her infancy. Thank you for caring me as I grew spiritually strong. I thank you for the plans that you have established for me. I know they are good, even if at times I experience unpleasantness, I know that I must experience growing pain. You are truly a remarkable, loving God. I put *all* my trust in the redeeming blood of Jesus, my Lord and Savior.

Isaiah 55:9 (KJV)
> For as the heavens are higher than the earth, so are my ways higher than your ways, and my thoughts than your thoughts.

Jeremiah 29:11 (KJV)
> For I know the thoughts that I think toward you, saith the Lord, thoughts of peace, and not of evil, to give you an expected end.

JANUARY 10

God is weaning me from all of my human dependencies. He wants my total dependence on Him. No matter what happens, I must keep my eyes on Him and trust Him even when I do not understand the process. I think about Joseph and all the troubles he had to endure; though he didn't understand, he kept his trust in God, knowing there was a bigger plan. He knew that God knew what he didn't; God had a plan to prosper him and his birth family. Though in a dark place, he kept his faith in God. You may not see what God is doing, and oftentimes we tend to place blame on the adversary, not knowing God is behind the scene working things out for our good. It may even appear as though He has left you, but don't be moved by what you see; only be moved by your faith in God. He will not allow anything to separate you from Him. When you falter in your strength, He is there carrying you and keeping you in perfect peace. Trust Him to catch you if you should fall. He will not leave you, nor will He forsake you. He will be with you even until the end of time, as He said in His word. He cannot lie.

Deuteronomy 33:27 (KJV)
> The eternal God is thy refuge, and underneath are the everlasting arms: and he shall thrust out the enemy from before thee; and shall say, Destroy them.

January 11

Peace is one of God's greatest gifts, without it, we suffer greatly. Life brings about tribulations, sufferings, and pain; the Holy Spirit gives us love, joy, and peace in the midst of our circumstances. He gives us hope in Christ Jesus, knowing that this experience is but for a moment and it shall pass. He gives me patience to weather the storm and building my faith as I struggle through it. Jesus left us His peace, not as the world gives, but unconditional peace that no matter what I'm faced with, I can use my gift of peace. My access card, which is the Holy Spirit, has many perks that comes along with it and has an unlimited balance. I thank you, Lord, that no matter what is going on around me, what hills or valleys I must go through, I can face them with my head held high because of the peace and security of knowing you and you knowing me well enough to trust me with the challenge so that I might bring forth much fruit. Whatever be the tide, I know it's not just for my growth but also that I might help others who are going through it also. Thank you for Holy Spirit and the fringe benefits of peace that He has given me.

John 16:33 (KJV)
> These things I have spoken unto you, that in me ye might have peace. In the world ye shall have tribulation: but be of good cheer; I have overcome the world.

JANUARY 12

As a personal trainer gets the physical body strengthen and in shape day after day, so is it with the spiritual man; it is renewed and strengthen daily by the various trials and tribulations. As I walk through life's struggles, I know that I'm never alone. We walk hand in hand, communing as we walk, and I focus on your glorious face as you coach me alone the rough spots in the road of life. You push me to keep close to you, whispering in my ear, "You can do it. You will go through. You are the very image of me, and there are no failures in me.

Failure is not an option when holding my hand and focusing on my glory and not the problem, (adversary). I know the failure is in me when I choose to let go of your hand and run away because of fear of the unknown future or when I'm distracted by an intriguing view alone the way. Even in those times, you remain the same. With outstretched arms you chasten me to come back; you never leave me. As a father patiently awaits his wayward child to come back home, you patiently bear with me in my folly, knowing I had to learn the lesson.

Each experience I encounter is for my making, whether good, bad, or indifferent, I'm better, wiser, and stronger because of the challenges I faced. In you, Lord, I have peace, knowing that I am the very image of you and because of you, I am victorious in all things, even in my failures (weakness), I'm victorious because it was a lesson learned, I'm wiser because of it. All the day long I will praise and worship you. You are my life, through Jesus Christ, and the power of your Holy Spirit that reside in me. I love you Lord!

Prayer: I independently give my hand to you, Lord, as you reach your hand out to me. I totally depend on your guidance as a child trusts his or her father, blindly unaware of where or what is before them. I trust the path you have set for me, never to harm me but to help me. Even when the road is rocky, dirty, and long, I know you are taking me through and I will endure hard times as a good soldier. I won't complain.

Psalm 73:23-24 (KJV)
> Nevertheless I am continually with thee: thou hast holden me by my right hand. [24] Thou shalt guide me with thy counsel, and afterward receive me to glory.

JANUARY 13

A life without trouble sounds great and perfect; however, that's not reality. If we suffer with Him we shall also reign with Him. God never promised us a life free of trouble. As a matter of fact, He lets us know, "that our afflictions will be many, but He will deliver us." That was a promise that He made to children— we are His children, and that was a personal promise He made to us. If you ever experience walking into a dark place, searching for light or a glimmer of something that's visible, that is when we can experience blind faith, trusting that in this life we will have dark moments, but as long as we trust God, hold His hand, and never let go, we will not have to search for the light. He is that light and knows exactly what is before us. When we bump into things or maybe even trip and fall, that's simply because we let go of His hand, lost our path and our sight.

We must depend on the God for our vision; He see what we can't see. He knows what's around the curve and what's on the road ahead. We must trust Him with every ounce of our being, knowing that He is in total control. Even when it seems that He isn't and that He is not listening, it's only a test. During the test, He must remain silent so that you and Holy Spirit can handle it together. He knows you can and will pass the test. It may not be with flying colors, but you passed and learned the lesson.

Prayer: Thank you, Father, for teaching, leading, and directing me through the trials of this life. In Jesus' name. Amen.

John 16:33 (KJV)
> These things I have spoken unto you, that in me ye might have peace. In the world ye shall have tribulation: but be of good cheer; I have overcome the world.

JANUARY 14

Where shall I go to hide from the Lord, if I should make my bed in the valley you are there, if I go to Mount Everest, my God is still there. The question is, why would I want to hide from my God? Instead I should be seeking after His face. Even when I mess up, He is there, beckoning me to come back, not to run further from Him. The face of the Lord is all around us; all things are naked before Him. When we sin willfully after knowing the truth, there remains no other sacrifice. God paid the ultimate sacrifice by giving His son as atonement for me.

Prayer: I'm thankful that you are ever-present in my life, though I may fall short of your glory, I have nowhere else to go. You are my strength and my protection. I will bless your name all the day long, and in you, you only, will I put my trust. I will continue to seek your face each day, as you grant me brand new mercies to face the day with endless possibilities in you.

Psalm 139:1-4 (KJV)
> O Lord, thou hast searched me, and known me. [2] Thou knowest my downsitting and mine uprising, thou understandest my thought afar off. [3] Thou compassest my path and my lying down, and art acquainted with all my ways. [4] For there is not a word in my tongue, but, lo, O Lord, thou knowest it altogether.

JANUARY 15

God doesn't dwell in clutter, confusion, nonsense, or anything that is out of order, even that of an unrenewed mind. When we focus on negative things that happened in our past as recent as a second earlier, we are shutting God out. Our minds must be renewed at all times. We must learn to eat the meat and throw away the bones (as my late father and friend would say). There is nothing that happened to you that God didn't ordain or permit. Have your human moment and move past it. Think on things that are lovely and positive, things that will help and not hurt. If our minds are renewed constantly, we would not find ourselves in positions or places that are not characteristics of Christian behavior.

So you ask, "How do I renew my mind"? The answer is easy; began by praising God throughout the day. That keeps you in His presence. Read or recite words of edification, knowing that God is in control of everything that relates to you. When trouble comes (and it will come), begin to examine the problem, taking note of your position in the problem: How did you contribute to it and what could you have done to prevent it? Take ownership of your part, make restitution, ask God for His forgiveness, and then keep it moving. By acknowledging your part in the problem, you have brought it to the forefront of your mind and spirit, thereby learning the lesson so that you will be wiser the next time and not fall prey to the trap of the adversary. There's always a lesson in everything, whether good or bad. We must become better because of it, not bitter. Our minds must be renewed constantly to stay spiritually healthy and alert.

Romans 12:2 (KJV) used
> And be not conformed to this world: but be ye transformed by the renewing of your mind, that ye may prove what is that good, and acceptable, and perfect will of God.

January 16

The eyes of the Lord are to and fro; he sees all and knows all that relates to me. I am His child, He loves me. Today is a blessing and tomorrow is not promised; all we have is now and our faith in the Lord God and Savior Jesus Christ. He knows all about me; he has ordained my life as it has pleased Him. I will not fear or worry about what shall be for I know my God holds the future. Therefore I will be thankful for my "present" today, and live while I have today for tomorrow isn't promised. If by reason of God's infinite wisdom and knowledge, I am blessed with tomorrow, I know He will take care of me and supply all of my needs—not some needs but all.

He sees my rising up and sitting my down; He has already made my way straight. I have faith in Him alone. It is in Him that I find favor with others, and it is in Him that I'm protected from a snare of the enemy. Even if I become shipwreck, destitute, naked, or sick, I can't look at the problem before me because it is temporary. I must deal with the problem and challenge myself to see and understand what I must learn from this, is it patience, love, or trust? All the time I believe that this, too, shall pass and thank God for the blessings that are to come. I will trust the Lord with all that is within me; when it seems my faith fails, He will coach me, push me, and show me a supernatural encounter that my faith will withstand whatever comes. He continues to prove His love for me, even when I feel that I don't deserve it.

I love you, Lord, for loving and caring for me, despite me and my human frailties.

Romans 8:31 (KJV)
> What shall we then say to these things? If God be for us, who can be against us?

JANUARY 17

God is saying, "Come to me for rest." your weariness and fatigue create a prime opportunity for Him. When you have gone seemingly the last mile and can't go any further, it is then that God wants us to trust totally and completely on Him. Most of the time we do the total opposite; we fail to trust Him and get upset or disappointed with Him and decide to go at it alone and on our own. Guess what? We fail miserably every time, and we also failed the test in our spiritual growth.

We fail to realize that with each problem, God and God is our only solution as Christians. We must not faint at a test we must go through and pass, lest we have to take it again. With each test that we pass, we grow. The problems — I like to refer to them as challenges — we face are not just for us, but that we might be a help to someone else, who might encounter the same.

God knows everything that concerns us. We must be obedient to His commands and leave the consequences to Him. He is faithful and just, and when we fight against Him, turn our backs to Him, disobey Him, and so on, we are only hurting ourselves and stumping our spiritual growth. It saddens the heart of our Father God to see us in such a contrite spirit. Go to Him; know that He is always waiting with outstretched arms to hold us tight. He knows us better than we know ourselves, He knows and feels our pains, hurts, sorrow, and disappointments, even before we do. He hurts when we hurts, but it's just like going through a sickness or injury of some sort. In order to feel better or be healed, you must endure some pain, but after the surgery is over, you began to recover and feel better.

We must take all our struggles to the Lord and know whatever the prognosis is, God is and has the remedy for you. You will come through victoriously if you look to Him only and be obedient to His word, fighting the good fight of faith. God is a rewarder for those who seek Him continuously.

Romans 8:28 (KJV)
> And we know that all things work together for good to them that love God, to them who are the called according to his purpose.

Prayer: Lord, I love you, and in you I will trust, knowing you know what is best for me. I don't. When my strength fails, I will fall gently into your arms and rest as you carry me through. In Jesus' name through the power of your Holy Spirit that fills my soul. Amen.

JANUARY 18

It's funny how we are always so busy doing this and that, going here and there and just everywhere, and before long the hours are far spent and the day is done. How much of the day did God receive? How many times out of our busy day did we remember to consult Him? Some of the things we end up doing is fruitless and could have been put off or not done. Can't you see that our busyness is by design? It doesn't just happen, or shall I say, we shouldn't just let it happen. I truly believe that nothing is by happenstance but by design.

Today is a gift; take time to be thankful for the gift, not in word only but in the things that you do. Take time to minister to the needs of others, by doing so you are ministering unto the Lord. He has ordained you for such a time as this. Don't spend all your time doing this and that; instead give yourself to God and be used by Him. If you are willing, he is more than able to perform it. Take some of the precious time that He has given you and give some back to Him. The word declares if you have help the lesser you have helped Him and you shall be rewarded for the deeds done in this life. Give God your time; allow Him to speak and you obey so that you will prove what that acceptable will of God is for your life. Your life isn't yours, but it belongs to Him; let Him use you for the glory and honor that He so richly deserves.

Luke 10:41-42 (KJV)
> And Jesus answered and said unto her, Martha, Martha, thou art careful and troubled about many things: [42] But one thing is needful: and Mary hath chosen that good part, which shall not be taken away from her.

JANUARY 19

When I think of all that Jesus endured and how He reacted to the pressure of it all, my dark valleys are nothing in comparison to His.

During the less trying times, the days are filled with joy and gladness and a little sunshine illuminates my surroundings. However, on those more darker days, when all things around me are dark, gloomy, and very heavy, it is then when I can see clearly the work of my Lord as He is keeping, leading, guiding, directing me out of that dark valley. It is then when I know He is right there with me, and at times He's even carrying me through that dark place of my day and those to come.

As we pass through the trials, storms, and tribulations, I'm totally aware of the fact that my God is passing through them with me. I'm never alone. Even when it feels like total solitude and heaviness on my shoulder that makes my knees buckle underneath me, He is right there.

It is the dark times of my life where God gets the most glory because I know as well as others who knows me that if it had not been for the Lord who is on my side, where would I be? I can do all things through Christ, as Romans 8:28 states, and without Him I could do nothing—I am nothing.

As we pass through (me and Jesus), I'm totally dependent on His strength, wisdom, and knowledge. I'm not that smart in and of myself, so I give all the glory to God for all the victories we won and the ones I have yet to win in and through Him.

God is good to me and so good for me.

Hebrews 12:3 (KJV)
> For consider him that endured such contradiction of sinners against himself, lest ye be wearied and faint in your minds.

January 20

Each day and every hour of the day, right down to the very second, God is with you. He loves the fact that we not only welcome His presence but we also acknowledge His face and welcome Him in our space. He is our very present help in our time of need. Therefore I will not fear trouble or run from trials. He tenderly guides me through as we pass the test before us. If tomorrow should not come, I trust that today I have fulfilled all that my God had for in store for me. He is my beginning and my completion of life. We must trust Him with our lives, knowing that He holds us in His arms. He is always with us and as long as we keep our focus on Him, we will never go astray. God is love, and we must love like Him every day and know that love casts out fear.

Isaiah 41:13 (KJV)
> For I, the Lord thy God, will hold thy right hand, saying unto thee, Fear not; I will help thee.

January 21

With God nothing is impossible; the sky is the limit. When I say sky, I mean Heaven, the throne of God. God is able to do anything but fail. We must know that He is our life, so no matter what was behind, what is ahead, or what we face today, God is in control and He knows what is best for us. He is our source and our strength; we shall soar on wings as eagles. Trust His love for us to prevail against all odds. Those valleys, hills, and deepest sea experiences are under His control, and we will pass safely through in His arms.

Rest in the comfort of knowing that during the times of trouble He shall guide you. Always look to Him, and take the time to make time for Him and His council. He's never far away. He can and will do the impossible. Through Him, our possibilities are endless. I will not set limits or boundaries on His power and strength.

As David defeated Goliath, we, too, are defeating the Philistines each day. We are blinded to some of the things He protects us from. He is here, waiting patiently for us to realize His presence and His goodness toward us. Stop putting the Trinity in confinement; He is in full operation in our daily lives. Give Him the love, honor, respect, and recognition He so deserves.

Psalm 23:1-4 (KJV)
> The Lord is my shepherd; I shall not want. [2] He maketh me to lie down in green pastures: he leadeth me beside the still waters. [3] He restoreth my soul: he leadeth me

in the paths of righteousness for his name's sake. [4] Yea, though I walk through the valley of the shadow of death, I will fear no evil: for thou art with me; thy rod and thy staff they comfort me.

JANUARY 22

The quiet times are when we can hear God's voice clearly. He wants to speak to you one on one. He wants to build the relationship that has been established. Don't always see those still times as negative. During our bed of affliction, unemployment, lack transportation, know that God is right there, affording you the time to have intimacy with Him, time for Him to really show and prove Himself to you in ways you never thought possible. Avail yourself to Him, at least meet Him halfway, not with complaints, disappointment, or defeat, but with open heart, ears, and arms. He wants you to want Him, not just to need Him. Make the time of stillness count, grow in that season as never before, and see your relationship with God transform to a higher more intimate level. And he said unto me, My grace is sufficient for thee: for my strength is made perfect in weakness. Most gladly therefore will I rather glory in my infirmities, that the power of Christ may rest upon me.

JANUARY 23

God is with me; that promise is all I need to survive. Never fool yourself into thinking you can go it alone. You can try it, but you will fail every time. Give God the opportunity to reveal His holy presence with us. He is our very present help in our times of trouble, sorrow, adversity, loneliness, and so on. Talk to Him constantly; whenever you feel alone, call the name of Jesus, the holy one. You'll see that He'll answer every time. Not only has God promised to be with us now, but He said forever more. I constantly say that loved ones will leave you, but God has promised never to leave us. Even in our stubborn moments, He is right there, awaiting our humble hearts and correct tone before He will act on our behalf. He only wants the love and respect He deserves.

Take time to allow His presence to be known every day of your life, arise to commune with Him, and lie down in sweet communion with Him, for He has promised, that He is with you. He is God, and He cannot lie.

Psalm 73:23-26 (KJV)
> Nevertheless I am continually with thee: thou hast holden me by my right hand. [24] Thou shalt guide me with thy counsel, and afterward receive me to glory. [25] Whom have I in heaven but thee? and there is none upon earth that I desire beside thee. [26] My flesh and my heart faileth: but God is the strength of my heart, and my portion for ever.

JANUARY 24

Trust and don't worry, be thankful, and don't complain, God wants our trust in all things throughout the day. The choice is ours, God never make us do anything, and He created us free morale being. In as much as He created us to make choices, He still wants us to come to trust Him with every ounce of our being. When we choose to trust God, we are actually submitting to His will, acknowledging Him as Lord over our lives and leaving all consequences to Him.

How can we not choose to give God preeminence of our lives? We go through much sickness, pain, and suffering because we choose to go it alone. Yes, we suffer through and hopefully learn the lesson in trusting God when He works on our behalf. Oh what needless pains we bear all because we do not carry everything, not some things, but everything to our God in prayer. We have this blessed assurance that if God be for us, it does not matter if this entire world is against us. We are in a win-win situation.

Prayer: Lord I thank you for being Lord of my life, and when things seems not to go favorably for us, we trust your plan. Just as Pastor preached on "A New Thing" yesterday, help us to accept the new things you have put before us and stop dwelling on what was. You are Lord of our tomorrow. Lord, I trust you, and I thank you for who you are, what you are, and who will be to me. I accept new things.

Colossians 2:6–7 (KJV)
> As ye have therefore received Christ Jesus the Lord, so walk ye in him: [7] Rooted and built up in him, and stablished in the faith, as ye have been taught, abounding therein with thanksgiving.

January 25

I will sit still and see the salvation of the Lord in all things. Though I know the Lord in His power, authority, and majesty now, I have even more to look forward to in paradise. His ecstasy will be reveal in its totality. Right now I experience Him through the word and through His Holy Spirit, but the future is even more glorious because it is then I shall see Him face to face in all His glory.

Nothing in this world is worth me missing out on such a glorious experience and life everlasting. This world is the Lord and everything that dwells here, so why should I be distracted when the enemy takes the things of God and tempts me to go against Him?

Anything you put before Him is idol worshipping; it's demonic. Just as a spouse would be furious about an unfaithful spouse, imagine how our God must feel when we commit idolatry.

He has given us everything, His life for our souls and life in abundance. He loves us just that much.

Ephesians 3:16–19 (KJV)
> That he would grant you, according to the riches of his glory, to be strengthened with might by his Spirit in the inner man; [17] That Christ may dwell in your hearts by faith; that ye, being rooted and grounded in love, [18] May be able to comprehend with all saints what is the breadth, and length, and depth, and height; [19] And to

know the love of Christ, which passeth knowledge, that ye might be filled with all the fulness of God.

January 26

With the Lord, I can do all things. As I focus on the road and path the God has paved for me, I will continue each step in faith, knowing that He is near and has purposes each step. I will trust in Him in each step, not knowing exactly where the path will lead, but knowing there is victory ahead. As long as I keep my focus on Him, I will stay the course. In Him I believe I shall not stumble, and I will not fall nor faint for He keeps me in perfect peace as I keep my eyes, heart, and mind on Him, and His will for my life. There is nothing concerning me that He doesn't already know, from my genes to my eternity with Him. I shall fulfill His purpose through and in me. He is everything and I looked to Him for all things.

Psalm 37:3-4 (KJV)
Trust in the Lord, and do good; so shalt thou dwell in the land, and verily thou shalt be fed. [4] Delight thyself also in the Lord; and he shall give thee the desires of thine heart.

Lord, I ask for wisdom to lead your people and give a just weight. I ask for knowledge just as yours and not that of man, that I may know how to give words of knowledge that will grow each of the people you place in my life. I ask for love, agape love, that I might love as you love, not with any respect for one but not for the other.

JANUARY 27

My life is totally in Christ. All that I do or say is with the thought of Christ in my life, the Holy Spirit taking charge and bringing into captivity the things that are not righteous. Because He lives, I live, and I will discuss every thought with Him, I know that He delights in the good, while He takes care of the bad. It's all good when you think about it. If it appears to be something bad, God works it out for the good. I'm so glad that God sent His son Jesus into this world as a ransom for the sins I committed. I joy in that He lives because I can now live free from sin and die without the sting of death.

Prayer: Wonderful, loving Savior, I thank you for dying that I might live. I thank you for helping all my weaknesses and infirmities. I now know I can conquer all challenges through the power of Holy Spirit who dwells on the inside of me. It is Jesus' name that I commit this prayer unto my God.

Acts 2:28 (KJV)
> Thou hast made known to me the ways of life; thou shalt make me full of joy with thy countenance.

JANUARY 28

Just take a moment to think about yourself: where you've been, what you've done, what's your plans for the future. Even when you look at your past, you could have never fathom the things that you had to endure, they were not all planned. Life happens, and no matter how we plan to control, we can't have total control. However, we know the One who has total control, who knows your ending from the beginning. It is He who has chosen you and already knows all there is to know about you. People seek mediums and all types of sorcery just to get a glimpse of what the future holds. We know the One who holds our future; let's consult Him about everything related to us — our desires, plans, needs, and even those thoughts that seemingly pop up from nowhere and take our focus from Him. Talk to the Master Mind behind everything — Our Lord and Savior.

Psalm 139:1-4 (KJV)
> O Lord, thou hast searched me, and known me. [2] Thou knowest my downsitting and mine uprising, thou understandest my thought afar off. [3] Thou compassest my path and my lying down, and art acquainted with all my ways. [4] For there is not a word in my tongue, but, lo, O Lord, thou knowest it altogether.

JANUARY 29

I give this day to you to help, hold, mold, shape, and make me according to your will. I desire you with every ounce of my being. I can face today knowing I'm not alone and that whatever be the tide, I know you will take care of me. I trust you and all your majesty and glory. I know that you care for me and all that concerns me. I feel your presence in my soul, and it envelopes me totally. I know with my whole heart, mind, and soul that we are one, and you are my soulmate. In you I put my trust; as I trust you to bring me through, my faith increases, and my patience is increased, displaying a boldness in the security of our connection. Our souls are tied.

Psalm 63:7–8 (KJV)
> Because thou hast been my help, therefore in the shadow of thy wings will I rejoice. [8] My soul followeth hard after thee: thy right hand upholdeth me.

JANUARY 30

I give my all to you and your desire is before me. I am constantly communicating with you, in my time of pain and sorrow as well as in joy and pleasures. I will tirelessly seek your will and not that of mine own. We are one, and I only want to do your will. When life challenges comes my way and try to distract me, I will look to you. When friends, family, and even foes comes against me, your face I will seek to take hold of and not the situation at hand. You are able to keep me in perfect peace; you are my strength and my salvation. I will make it through this with you, not without you. You have already given me the power to have, to be, and to do your will with exceedingly joy. I can't go wrong by doing what is right. I will do your will, seek you, and keep you always in the forefront.

Matthew 6:33 (KJV)
> But seek ye first the kingdom of God, and his righteousness; and all these things shall be added unto you.

January 31

This day is already planned out. God established it way before I started planning for it. He will take care of me and all that relates to me. I feel His security forces all around me, and goodness and mercy continually encamp about me.

Upon waking, ask God what His plans are for you today and to show you what steps to take. We have a constant consultant, the Holy Spirit. He is just anxiously waiting to help us. Don't forget to remember to talk with Him. Ask for His guidance for this day that was already established. What time we waste and mistakes we make when we go at it alone.

Matthew 6:34 (KJV)
> Take therefore no thought for the morrow: for the morrow shall take thought for the things of itself. Sufficient unto the day is the evil thereof.

TAKE AWAYS (NOTES)

FEBRUARY

Luke 6:27 KJV - [27] But I say unto you which hear, Love your enemies, do good to them which hate you.

FEBRUARY 1

There's so much going on in the world in which we live, and if we aren't careful, it could consume us so that we would be in constant fear and turmoil. Bad news seems to be the norm nowadays. We must put our trust in God, knowing that nothing catches Him by surprise. He is our protector, guide, and comforter; actually, He's everything we need, now and throughout eternity.

WORD FOR TODAY:

Psalm 91:10-11 (KJV)
There shall no evil befall thee, neither shall any plague come nigh thy dwelling. [11] For he shall give his angels charge over thee, to keep thee in all thy ways.

FEBRUARY 2

We are to be helpful one to another, so there should always be sufficiency in the body of Christ. We are one body, one family unit in Christ Jesus, and when one member has need, we are commissioned by God to aid them in obtaining what they need. God has blessed us so that we can bless others. Ministry is who we are, not just what we do when it's convenient or popular. Understanding that ministry is seeing a need and meeting it. That puts us on a daily mission to care for others.

WORD FOR TODAY:

Acts 4:32 (KJV)
> And the multitude of them that believed were of one heart and of one soul: neither said any of them that ought of the things which he possessed was his own; but they had all things common.

FEBRUARY 3

What God has for you, is for you; no one can take it away from you or have it because it's yours. Never be envious or jealous of anyone, which is sensual and evil and even demonic. We must rejoice in their gifts and blessings. God is the source in which all blessings comes. He blesses others just as He blesses us; what He has done for others, He will definitely do it for you. When we are envious and jealous, we block our own blessings. God tells us to rejoice with them that do rejoice. God knows the intent of our hearts. When our hearts are filled with love and is pure, we are excited when others do well.

Word for Today:

13 Who is wise and understanding among you? Let him show by good conduct that his works are done in the meekness of wisdom. 14 But if you have bitter envy and self-seeking in your hearts, do not boast and lie against the truth. 15 This wisdom does not descend from above, but is earthly, sensual, demonic. 16 For where envy and self-seeking exist, confusion and every evil thing are there.

February 4

Our God is Spirit and has declared that we *must* worship Him in spirit and truth. He is so worthy of our worship. He desires for us to come to Him and serve Him from our hearts, knowing that He first loved us and has been great to us. As we look back over our lives, it shouldn't be hard to see that He has always been there, protecting us from dangers that we see and the ones we didn't see. His love and grace draws us to Him. When you think about all that He has done, is doing, and will do, it makes you want to praise and worship Him. Only you know how good God has been to you; no praise team should have to make you get into worship.. We enter into His gates, the door of the church, rendering praise. Praise is not what we do, but who we are; we are Levites and Judah. God is worthy of all praise, glory, and honor. His divine nature is pure and holy; our worship is pure and holy.

Word for Today:

4:23
> "True worshipers will worship the Father in spirit and truth."

February 5

In the midst of the day, I will trust you and seek your presence. As I keep my mind on you, your peace envelopes me. You are my help and my protection from the storms and the rains. In you I will trust and not fear any snares that are set before me. Whether I understand it or not, I know that all things will work out for my good.

Psalm 46:1-2 (KJV)
> God is our refuge and strength, a very present help in trouble. [2] Therefore will not we fear, though the earth be removed, and though the mountains be carried into the midst of the sea.

February 6

There's a song I remember singing as I child "I will trust in the Lord, until I die." At that time I didn't understand exactly what it meant, not in its fullness, but it always stuck with me. No matter what situations we may face, keeping our trust only in God is key to a successful outcome. We must know that God will keep us, lead us, speak to us, and even carry us if we should get weak and feeble. His strength is made perfect in our weakness; it's then we have total reliance on Him and know beyond a shadow of doubt that it is God who worked it all out. Stay in God's presence and never forget to remember, He is always ready and available to us.

WORD FOR THE DAY:

Psalm 18:2 (KJV)
> The Lord is my rock, and my fortress, and my deliverer; my God, my strength, in whom I will trust; my buckler, and the horn of my salvation, and my high tower.

FEBRUARY 7

We are Christ's example in the earth before a godless generation of people who do not know Him. We must do what is right and stand on what's right and pleasing unto God. There's someone who will cross our paths at the right time, so we must be ready to give them a word and share the gospel of the good news of Jesus Christ our Savior. We must be apt to teach when convenient and when it's not, and we must always be sober and reverent in our behavior so that the word of God may not be blasphemed. Once we commit our lives to Him, we must be under His full control at all times.

WORD FOR THE DAY:

Titus 2:2-3
> Be sober, reverent, temperate, sound in faith, in love, in patience... teachers of good things.

February 8

Because He lives, we now live into eternal life, not after the fleshly manner but after the Spirit man. Now that my life is anew in Christ Jesus, I look to Him for direction for my life that is in and through Him. I ask for His help at any given moment. What I cannot do, He can and will do and perfect all that relates to me. I can face each new day, knowing that my God is in control, and in His presence I find the joy and peace, even in the midst of my storm.

Word for the Day:

Ephesians 2:6
> And hath raised us up together, and made us sit together in heavenly places in Christ Jesus.

February 9

I will praise you in my frequent trials, knowing that the trying of my faith works patience. I know that you will not put more on me than I'm able to handle. I will trust you in all my ways. For me to live is in you, and I will speak your word as words of encouragement.

Word for Today:

2 Corinthians 4:8–10 (KJV)
> We are troubled on every side, yet not distressed; we are perplexed, but not in despair; [9] Persecuted, but

not forsaken; cast down, but not destroyed; [10] Always bearing about in the body the dying of the Lord Jesus, that the life also of Jesus might be made manifest in our body.

2 Corinthians 4:7 (KJV)
But we have this treasure in earthen vessels, that the excellency of the power may be of God, and not of us.

FEBRUARY 10

Constructive criticism doesn't always feel good when given, but it is the best thing for us if given by the right person and in the right manner. We shouldn't despise or rejected good counsel, especially from our spiritual cover, neither from God. God has given us His word as a guide to a life of prosperity and good success. If we are apt to receive good instructions and obey them, we will do well, and God will bless us. It's immature to reject correction; you'll never learn neither grow. Always obey God's instructions and you will definitely reap His good. He blesses obedience.

WORD FOR THE DAY:

Proverbs 12:1
Whoever loves instruction loves knowledge, but he who hates correction is stupid.

Proverbs 13:18
> Poverty and shame will come to him who disdains correction, but he who regards a rebuke will be honored.

FEBRUARY 11

As the rain pours, the clouds cover the sun and the day seems so dark. I can still see the sun shining through your word as you have given me new life; your word is a light to my pathway. Throughout the day I will look to you for a clear path that will lead me continuously in the right direction. You are my compass; I depend on you to get me where I need to go. You are that light that shines within me.

WORD FOR THE DAY:

John 1:4–5 (KJV)
> In him was life; and the life was the light of men. [5] And the light shineth in darkness; and the darkness comprehended it not.

FEBRUARY 12

You're never alone. Even when emotions are making you feel as though you're by yourself, with no one understand and no one to depend on, God is with you and inside of you, comforting and keeping you. You must forever praise and delight yourself in His goodness and love for you. Because He lives, we live. There's nothing you can't do with God dwelling on the inside. He's empowering you to live as He would live to speak as He would speak, to love as He would love. As you render the sacrifice of praise, you will feel His presence and the weight of the world lifting from your soul.

Psalm 37:4 (KJV)
> Delight thyself also in the Lord; and he shall give thee the desires of thine heart.

FEBRUARY 13

The Lord is our peace; it is in Him that we live and have our being. Though troubled on every side, I find peace in my God, who will be my strong tower. There's no mountain too high or giant too strong for my Lord. When I am weak through human frailty, I depend on the Lord my God for strength and peace in the midst of the battle.

WORD FOR THE DAY:

John 20:19 (KJV)
> Then the same day at evening, being the first day of the week, when the doors were shut where the disciples were assembled for fear of the Jews, came Jesus and stood in the midst, and saith unto them, Peace be unto you.

FEBRUARY 14

God loved us from the beginning of creation and made a way for us to be saved from destruction. He made the plan of salvation so simple that all we have to do is believe. Man is the one to make it complex. All we are asked to do is believe that Jesus Christ is God in the flesh. He disrobed Himself, put on human flesh, and condemned sin in the flesh, becoming the lamb sacrifice. He was tempted just as we're are, but He didn't sin. Salvation is not something that you can purchase or earn, so accept Jesus' love and saving grace. Believe totally in Him and inherit eternal life.

Word for the Day:

John 3:16-18 KJV

[16] For God so loved the world, that he gave his only begotten Son, that whosoever believeth in him should not perish, but have everlasting life. [17] For God sent not his Son into the world to condemn the world; but that the world through him might be saved. [18] He that believeth on him is not condemned: but he that believeth not is condemned already, because he hath not believed in the name of the only begotten Son of God.

February 15

We never have to speak one single word about what we do to help others. God sees the generosity and kindness you share with His children. He will reward and acknowledge you before great men and women for your acts of love. It seems that everyone wants the glory and honor for what they do, but if you think about it, it's only by the blessings of God that you're able to do for others. When we help others, we are planting seeds that will generate a great harvest, and you'll never suffer lack. The law principle of sowing and reaping is as relevant now as it was in creation. God sees your good deeds, and He will give you the accolades that you deserve, so never boast. We do not need to boast about our Spirit-led good deeds or advertise the kind things we do that might otherwise be overlooked. God gives the only rewards that matter, and He keeps careful tally.

Word for the Day:

Matthew 6:4
> Your Father who sees in secret will Himself reward you openly.

February 16

In times when I'm stagnant due to unforeseen circumstances, sickness, or failed health, I will be glad in knowing God is there to hold me up, give me a word, and strengthen me during times of weakness or when my strength fails. God is more than enough for me and will keep me in perfect peace. I will be still and quiet and listen as He instructs me. He is my strength.

Word for the Day:

2 Corinthians 13:9 (KJV)
> For we are glad, when we are weak, and ye are strong: and this also we wish, even your perfection.

FEBRUARY 17

Change is inevitable. So long as we live, change will happen. Struggle becomes complacency, the norm, the familiar, and the comfort of where we are as we remain the same. We must trust that change is good when it relates to us as children of the most High. His plans for us are good; we will succeed in all that He has I store for us. He will withhold nothing good and righteous from us. We should embrace each new day, asking God for guidance in learning what is new so that it will benefit Him and bring more people into the newness of life.

WORD FOR THE DAY:

2 Corinthians 5:17 (KJV)
> Therefore if any man be in Christ, he is a new creature: old things are passed away; behold, all things are become new.

FEBRUARY 18

I have hope and a blessed assurance in knowing that no matter what happens to me or who hurt and disappoints me, God will never leave nor forsake me. He is forever with me, even until the end of my time here in the earth. Then He will receive me eternally in His Kingdom. I know that I'm never alone, even when my feelings dictates contrary feelings of loneliness. All I need to do is call upon the name of the Lord, who is my help and my strength, a very present help in my time of need. He takes me by my right hand and leads me as well as protects me. Lord, I thank you for never leaving nor forsaking me.

WORD FOR TODAY:

Psalm 73:23-26 (KJV)
> Nevertheless I am continually with thee: thou hast holden me by my right hand. [24] Thou shalt guide me with thy counsel, and afterward receive me to glory. [25] Whom have I in heaven but thee? and there is none upon earth that I desire beside thee. [26] My flesh and my heart faileth: but God is the strength of my heart, and my portion for ever.

FEBRUARY 19

My dependence on God grows more and more each day. As I realize that I'm not in control of my future, I find that God is. I'm the vehicle that He uses to accomplish His plan for me. He already knows my future, and I seek His face for direction for my life. With each new day, I'm empowered to do what He has

created me to do and to be whom He created me to be. As I pray for His will, I listen attentively to His voice for His instructions and follow. If I'm not sure or need help, I simply ask, conversing with Him throughout the day. He knows what I have need of. He's just waiting for me to communicate that to Him. Pray consistently throughout the day in simple short sweet prayers and praise.

WORD FOR THE DAY:

John 16:24 (KJV)
> Hitherto have ye asked nothing in my name: ask, and ye shall receive, that your joy may be full.

FEBRUARY 20

You are my peace, God; in you I find calm of spirit and soul. I will look inward to your peace in your dwelling place and be thankful for that secret place. You are my peace and comfort and I'm forever thankful.

WORD FOR THE DAY:

Colossians 3:15 (KJV)
> And let the peace of God rule in your hearts, to the which also ye are called in one body; and be ye thankful.

FEBRUARY 21

I'm so lost without God; I can't imagine what my life would be without Him. As I train my thoughts to focus on Him and *all* His goodness toward me, there's no other place I'd rather be. When problems surface, I put them to the back of my mind and began to ask God for the solution, which He already has. It keeps me focused on God and not the troubles that arise. They are a distraction to the inner peace that God has given me. I'm journeying in this life, so what I know is that my Father cares for me. He chose me, and therefore, no evil shall over take His child. I'm a child of the most High, and He loves me more than anyone else. I look to you, my God, and I will think of your goodness to me. I will not grumble or complain about what I don't have because I'm so thankful for the things that I do have. Knowing there's no good thing you will ever withhold from me. I will have just what you want me to have.

Word for the Day:

Psalm 141:8 (KJV)
> But mine eyes are unto thee, O God the Lord: in thee is my trust; leave not my soul destitute.

1 Peter 5:7 (KJV)
> Casting all your care upon him; for

February 22

Every day we should find ourselves asking God to create in us a clean heart and to renew a right spirit within us. There are many things that will distract us to ultimately take our focus off of God and His directions for us. It's easy to react to the flesh by the various devices the enemy throws our way. We as believers want more than anything to obey and please God. Our conscience is tender toward God's

commandments, because at the point of conversion, His Spirit and our spirits became one. Now the Holy Spirit bears witness of the truth of God's word and keeps us from practicing sin. I encourage you to keep your mind on spiritual things, and your heart will be continually compelled to do what is right and pleasing unto God. You may ask what you will and it shall be given unto you.

Word for the Day:

Psalm 51:10 (KJV)
> Create in me a clean heart, O God; and renew a right spirit within me.

February 23

I will not fall into the pit of despair or feeling sorry for myself. Things happen in life that are pleasant or make you feel that you have been dealt a bad hand. It's your hand nonetheless, and God has a plan set for you. The hand that looks to be bad will actually be the best hand for you. Know that God is with you and for you, and there's nothing you can't conquer with God by our side. Be patience during your time of trouble, and God will see you through.

Word for the Day:

Hebrews 12:1-2 (KJV)
> Wherefore seeing we also are compassed about with so great a cloud of witnesses, let us lay aside every weight, and the sin which doth so easily beset us, and let us run with patience the race that is set before us, [2] Looking unto Jesus the author and finisher of our faith; who for the joy that was set before him endured the cross,

despising the shame, and is set down at the right hand of the throne of God.

FEBRUARY 24

As I awoke this morning, there was a feeling of dread and trepidation, which had to be as a result of a sleepless night. Unwanted, incomprehensible dreams invaded my peaceful sleep. Immediately, the Holy Spirit quickened me and reminded me of God's love and grace toward me. I woke up to new life and new mercies, and God's love started to invade the space of unwanted emotions. Where love is, hate, loneliness, fear, and depression have to leave. They certainly cannot take up residence in the same space. I thank God for His love and peace that fills me and the Holy Spirit who completely fills my soul. When emotions that are contradictory to the indwelling Holy Spirit tries to invade my temple, the Holy Spirit and God's love is right there to kick it out. Negativity shall not and will not prevail.

WORD FOR TODAY:

Ephesians 3:16-19 (KJV)
> That he would grant you, according to the riches of his glory, to be strengthened with might by his Spirit in the inner man; [17] That Christ may dwell in your hearts by faith; that ye, being rooted and grounded in love, [18] May be able to comprehend with all saints what is the breadth, and length, and depth, and height; [19] And to

know the love of Christ, which passeth knowledge, that ye might be filled with all the fulness of God.

FEBRUARY 25

To be thankful in all things is what God requires of us. He didn't have to do, but He did. Whatever the good is, God did it. Things could be worse. When negative thoughts invade my mind, I simply reflect on the goodness of God and all that He has done for me, and I just simply cannot complain. God is so good to me, and He is so good for me. When you petition the Lord in prayer about anything, begin to give Him thanks in advance, believing He can and will perform it according to His will. In everything be thankful.

WORD FOR TODAY:

Colossians 4:2 (KJV)
   Continue in prayer, and watch in the same with thanksgiving;

FEBRUARY 26

I will not worry about tomorrow, I don't know what it will bring, but I know who holds my future, and it is Him in whom I put my trust. He knows what I don't know. I totally depend on God's guidance each and every day.

Word for Today:

Deuteronomy 29:29 (KJV)
> The secret things belong unto the Lord our God: but those things which are revealed belong unto us and to our children forever, that we may do all the words of this law.

Psalm 32:8 (KJV)
> I will instruct thee and teach thee in the way which thou shalt go: I will guide thee with mine eye.

FEBRUARY 27

Be careful of the things you allow into your temple because at some point it will surface; it's extracted one way or another. The body is the temple in which Holy Spirit has taken residence. He cannot and will not dwell in an unclean temple, so be careful and prayerful about what we accept or allow through the eyes, ears, and mouth. Seek the Holy Spirit, and if any time you are uncomfortable or unsure, that means He is unsettled and does not want you to partake of it. Do not quench or override the Spirit because there are always consequences to pay. We have God's commandments to obey; also, we must be in tune with His voice so that we may know what is clean and unclean. If we don't feel condemnation, then we are not condemned, but if we know in our hearts that something is not right, do not do it, do not say it, and do not eat or drink it. Obey the unction of Holy Spirit. Disobedience is sin.

Word for the Day:

Matthew 15:16-18 (KJV)
> And Jesus said, Are ye also yet without understanding? [17] Do not ye yet understand, that whatsoever entereth in at the mouth goeth into the belly, and is cast out into the draught? [18] But those things which proceed out of the mouth come forth from the heart; and they defile the man.

1 John 3:19-22 (KJV)
> And hereby we know that we are of the truth, and shall assure our hearts before him. [20] For if our heart condemn us, God is greater than our heart, and knoweth all things. [21] Beloved, if our heart condemn us not, then have we confidence toward God. [22] And whatsoever we ask, we receive of him, because we keep his commandments, and do those things that are pleasing in his sight.

February 28

God is not interested in being mad nor punishing you. He's not a God that searches for the bad in order to come down harshly in His judgment. He is a loving, long-suffering God who delights in His love toward us. When He has to punish us, it's just as a parent says when disciplining their children, "This hurts me more than it hurts you." It hurts in ways that you as His child don't understand. His love for us supersedes that of any other. No one enjoys seeing their loved one in pain.

He has to discipline us in order for us to learn the lesson, so we will understand the consequences and not err in that way again. It is always to help and not to hurt.

WORD FOR TODAY:

Luke 6:37 (KJV)
> Judge not, and ye shall not be judged: condemn not, and ye shall not be condemned: forgive, and ye shall be forgiven:

John 3:16-17 (KJV)
> For God so loved the world, that he gave his only begotten Son, that whosoever believeth in him should not perish, but have everlasting life. [17] For God sent not his Son into the world to condemn the world; but that the world through him might be saved.

Proverbs 3:11-12 (KJV)
> [11] My son, despise not the chastening of the Lord; neither be weary of his correction: [12] For whom the Lord loveth he correcteth; even as a father the son in whom he delighteth.

TAKE AWAYS (NOTES)

MARCH

Joel 2:22 KJV - [22] Be not afraid, ye beasts of the field: for the pastures of the wilderness do spring, for the tree beareth her fruit, the fig tree and the vine do yield their strength.

MARCH 1

Even when death hits home, He keeps us in perfect peace. Yes, we cry and are saddened but at peace, knowing to be absent from the body is to be present with the Lord. I say death because that is the worst thing that could happen. However, through all my circumstances, He has kept me peacefully in His presence, comforting and whispering His word to me. Lord, I trust you with me.

WORD FOR TODAY:

Philippians 4:6 (KJV) Isaiah 26:3 (KJV)
 Thou wilt keep him in perfect peace, whose mind is stayed on thee: because he trusteth in thee.

MARCH 2

What an awesome God and Savior Jesus Christ. There's always a plan, nothing just happens. He continues to live in the earth through us. Once we accept Him into our lives, He leads and directs us to carry out His will in the earth. As a result, He rewards us with life everlasting. Each day I will allow His will to be done in and through me, knowing I'm fulfilling His purpose and plan for my life.

WORD FOR TODAY:

John 11:25 (KJV)
> Jesus said unto her, I am the resurrection, and the life: he that believeth in me, though he were dead, yet shall he live:

MARCH 3

It's so important for us to talk with the Lord and listen when He answers us. Many times the voices in our heads speak to us, and we don't quite know which voice is the Lord. However, if we take the time to communicate and listen, His voice is distinct. If you listen long and frequently, you will know His voice above all other voices. Spend time listening and obeying your shepherd, so you'll always distinguish between the voice of your master and the others.

Word for Today:

John 10:4 (KJV)
> And when he putteth forth his own sheep, he goeth before them, and the sheep follow him: for they know his voice.

March 4

It is what it is. If you can change it, change it; if not accept it, deal with it and keep moving. Pray for wisdom to know the things you can change and the things you can't. Many times we stress and worry about things needlessly, which leads to all sorts of health issues. Don't worry; trust God, and things will work out for your good.

Word for the Day:

Luke 12:25-26 (KJV)
> And which of you with taking thought can add to his stature one cubit? [26] If ye then be not able to do that thing which is least, why take ye thought for the rest?

March 5

How you see the problem is really the problem. You can befriend it and learn all there is to learn about this problem or see it as an enemy to fight against, never learning the lesson, which you are bound to repeat again. See God and yourself bigger than the problem and begin to thank God for learning the lesson.

God uses different problems, situations, and challenges to make us stronger and much wiser. Praise Him through it all.

Word for Today:

Romans 8:28 (KJV)
> And we know that all things work together for good to them that love God, to them who are the called according to his purpose.

March 6

The unforeseen and seen challenges of today overwhelmed me as I gave thought to how I would juggle all that is before me. There are only twenty-four hours in which to do them all. God is time; He already knows my limitations as a mortal being, so I will depend on Him to help me formulate the demands of my day. He will keep me in perfect peace. I will feel comfort as He holds me by His right hand. He is more powerful than our minds can imagine.

Word for Today:

Psalm 63:7–8 (KJV)
> Because thou hast been my help, therefore in the shadow of thy wings will I rejoice. [8] My soul followeth hard after thee: thy right hand upholdeth me.

MARCH 7

Our God can do exceedingly above anything you could think of. So make your request known unto God, whatever your desire and or need; just ask, and He will willingly grant your requests. There's nothing our Father will not do for us. A cattle on a thousand hills is ours. While we ask for the things of the natural, always ask for the spiritual. God will give us wisdom, knowledge, and understanding of His word. As you grow in the word, your knowledge and understanding of all you can obtain will be clearer to us.

WORD FOR THE DAY:

Psalm 37:3-4 (KJV)
> Trust in the Lord, and do good; so shalt thou dwell in the land, and verily thou shalt be fed. [4] Delight thyself also in the Lord; and he shall give thee the desires of thine heart.

MARCH 8

You are stronger than you know; no, not in and of yourself, but through the power of Holy Spirit, you can move mountains. Whatever your struggle is, whatever the challenge, you are more than able to endure. Think about it: God said you are more than a conqueror. That means success in every challenge you face. You can and will make it through. You are a victor and not a victim. God will give you just what you need to make it through.

Word for the Day:

1 Chronicles 16:11 (KJV)
Seek the Lord and his strength, seek his face continually.

March 9

When the day seems a bit strained and very busy, take the time to get in God's presence where you'll find peace and serenity. It will keep you from falling apart; it's a breather, a second breath, fresh wind for another run of the day. Take the time to share with others the peace that keeps you throughout the day. God gives you love, joy, and kindness, so distribute it to others to help them along their way.

Word for the Day:

Galatians 5:22 (KJV)
But the fruit of the Spirit is love, joy, peace, longsuffering, gentleness, goodness, faith,

March 10

Everything I do have done or will do in the future, God has divinely orchestrated, yes, even eternity. It's important for us not to focus on negative situations but look at the lessons learned through them. You came through with Jesus holding you by the hand. You may have some scraps or wounds to serve as a reminder to not repeat again.

Word for Today:

Psalm 37:23-24 (KJV)
> The steps of a good man are ordered by the Lord: and he delighteth in his way. [24] Though he fall, he shall not be utterly cast down: for the Lord upholdeth him with his hand.

MARCH 11

It's never about me, but it's all about Jesus. His sovereign power and Lordship in our lives and in the earth. I will not be moved by the things my eyes see; I will only be moved by what I believe my God can do, and He can do anything but fail. His power is unlimited and innumerable. I will trust in Him and no man. It's His power that dwells on the inside of me. My faith is what carries me through each trial I face, knowing God can bring me through, and yes, He will.

Word for Today:

2 Corinthians 5:7 (KJV)
> For we walk by faith, not by sight.

Galatians 5:25 (KJV)
> If we live in the Spirit, let us also walk in the Spirit.

March 12

"I will trust you, Lord" are the words that He continues to put on my lips. No matter what comes my way, "Lord I trust you; in you only do I trust to do what only you can, working things out for my good." I will wait as Job did, each day. Little confirmations come my way to let me know you are listening and you answer my prayers. It's remarkable to see you work. It's amazing how God works things out and it's all so divinely orchestrated that you know that you know Lord I trust you!

Word for Today:

John 14:1 (KJV)
> Let not your heart be troubled: ye believe in God, believe also in me.

Psalm 27:14 (KJV)
> Wait on the Lord: be of good courage, and he shall strengthen thine heart: wait, I say, on the Lord.

March 13

The Lord will keep you in perfect peace if you keep your mind on Him. When Jesus is bigger than your problems, then you'll have no problem staying the course in faith. Just remember to keep Him first, knowing He is in control of *all* things, and surely things will work out for your good. Be joyous because that's good news.

WORD FOR TODAY:

John 16:33 (KJV)
> These things I have spoken unto you, that in me ye might have peace. In the world ye shall have tribulation: but be of good cheer; I have overcome the world.

MARCH 14

It's amazing when I think of just how amazing God's love is toward us. We are so accustomed to giving and receiving, it's hard to believe that all God wants is for us to believe that His Son Jesus Christ was born, died, and resurrected for us. He gave His Son freely. Jesus willingly gave His life to pardon, or pay, our sin debt. All we have to do is believe and receive. Wow, there's nothing attached or hidden agendas, and it's all for our good, just because He loved us that much. We have eternal life that will cost us no monetary substance, just belief. How can we escape perdition if we neglect so great of salvation?

WORD FOR THE DAY:

Ephesians 3:17–19 (KJV)
> That Christ may dwell in your hearts by faith; that ye, being rooted and grounded in love, [18] May be able to comprehend with all saints what is the breadth, and length, and depth, and height; [19] And to know the love of Christ, which passeth knowledge, that ye might be filled with all the fulness of God.

Psalm 46:10 (KJV)
> Be still, and know that I am God: I will be exalted among the heathen, I will be exalted in the earth.

MARCH 15

We have for some reason pictured God as this huge strong integrity just waiting to punish us when we do wrong ... on the contrary – God doesn't punish us, we punish ourselves; it's the consequences of our actions. We inflict pain, grief and agony on ourselves when we failed to do what is right. Our God is a God of love and desire to do is good and not harm. His love and goodness toward us should be encouragement to us to do what is right in His sight. When we are saved and filling God's word, we can ask what we will and it shall be given. We can knock on Heavens door in prayer and He will open the door for us. Doors that no man can shut. We have access that we can use whenever needed. God constantly rejoices over us, He brags about us, He never I mean never desire to do us harm. Harm comes as a result of our disobedience. Obey God and leave all consequence to Him. You will always have a successful outcome.

WORD FOR TODAY:

Zephaniah 3:17 (KJV)
> The Lord thy God in the midst of thee is mighty; he will save, he will rejoice over thee with joy; he will rest in his love, he will joy over thee with singing.

MARCH 16

My circumstances will not control me, but I will control every situation and circumstances with God alone. I will keep my focus on Him, and He will give me perfect peace. I will call upon my Lord, and He will strengthen my soul. His strength is made perfect in my weakness. I will rise above my issues for truly, they are not mine, but the Lord's.

WORD FOR TODAY:

John 16:33 (KJV)
> These things I have spoken unto you, that in me ye might have peace. In the world ye shall have tribulation: but be of good cheer; I have overcome the world.

MARCH 17

When you feel alone and no one seems to understand you, think again. We serve a God who actually created you from the dust of the earth. He also established your heart. He knows all there is to know about you, so you need not be ashamed or embarrassed. Nothing takes God by surprise and never will. He knows what you don't know about your future, so talk to Him.

Word for Today:

Psalm 139:1-4 (KJV)
> O Lord, thou hast searched me, and known me. [2] Thou knowest my downsitting and mine uprising, thou understandest my thought afar off. [3] Thou compassest my path and my lying down, and art acquainted with all my ways. [4] For there is not a word in my tongue, but, lo, O Lord, thou knowest it altogether.

March 18

Every day, all through the day, tell the Lord you trust Him. No matter what you are going through, God is able to do abundantly above what any man can do. All things are working out for your good. His thoughts toward us are good. So trust God in everything; don't try to figure it out. God has already worked it out. We have His word, His promises, and they stand sure. God cannot lie. So pray, obey, and trust Him with c that pertains to you. God can and He will do it just for you. He loves us unconditionally. Yes, man has and will continue to let you down, but God never will. Trust Him and be blessed.

Word for Today:

Psalm 84:12 (KJV)
> O Lord of hosts, blessed is the man that trusteth in thee.

MARCH 19

Upon waking and starting your day, ask God to lead, guide, and direct His vessel in the way He would have it. Be aware of God's presence with you and in you. You are His, and He is yours, so ask God to order each of your steps by His word. When we go at it alone, we will mess up every time. Allow God to be in charge of what you do, what you think, and what you say. He is the author of your autobiography. He knows what is best for you.

WORD FOR TODAY:

Romans 8:1-2 (KJV)
> 1 There is therefore now no condemnation to them which are in Christ Jesus, who walk not after the flesh, but after the Spirit.
>
> 2 For the law of the Spirit of life in Christ Jesus hath made me free from the law of sin and death.

1 Corinthians 6:19-20 (KJV)
> What? know ye not that your body is the temple of the holy Ghost which is in you, which ye have of God, and ye are not your own? [20] For ye are bought with a price: therefore glorify God in your body, and in your spirit, which are God's.

March 20

Lord I'm so thankful for the gift of your Holy Spirit that has united with my spirit. He has taken preeminence within me; he continues to lead, guide, teach, and most of all, keep me. When I'm distracted or confused, if I just remember to call on the Holy Spirit, I will overcome any challenges that I encounter. Lord, I thank you for freedom from sin and hang ups. You have given me a peace and freedom that I don't even understand. You are my keeper from now until eternity.

Word for Today:

2 Corinthians 5:5 (KJV)
> Now he that hath wrought us for the selfsame thing is God, who also hath given unto us the earnest of the Spirit.

March 21

When we focus on God and the power, all power that He possess, our possibilities are endless. Through Him we can do all things without fear; we can conquer the impossible and reach far beyond the sky. Fear is a word that we should not entertain; it is a spirit of evil which God didn't give us, so we should not gravitate to it, nor entertain it. We are His workmanship, created for His service. Let us stand as bold soldiers in God's army, giving our weaknesses to Him and exchanging it for His strength. Declare I can reach the unattainable, I can conquer the mighty, and I can have joy continuously while I fight the good fight of faith.

Our journey is one that has already been prepared for us by our God. Trust Him and take time to enjoy the scenery along the way because all of it is His creation, and it's for our pleasure. I'm so happy that I found you and know you to be my everything.

Prayer: You, God, alone will I put my trust in; you are faithful and mighty. I will forever cling to you and love you with all my heart, with all my might, and with all of my strength. Through the power and anointing of Holy Spirit, in Jesus' name. Amen.

WORD FOR TODAY:

Isaiah 12:2 (KJV)
> [2} Behold, God is my salvation; I will trust, and not be afraid: for the Lord Jehovah is my strength and my song; he also is become my salvation.

MARCH 22

Even when things seems discombobulated, we must learn to trust God. That's only a diversion to keep us from focusing on God and His goodness. We must be thankful and constantly in a state of rejoicing. The Lord will lift every broken heart and contrite spirit. What better options do we have? Trust God.

Word for Today:

Philippians 4:4 (KJV)
   Rejoice in the Lord alway: and again I say, Rejoice.

Psalm 9:10 (KJV)
   [10] And they that know thy name will put their trust in thee: for thou, Lord, hast not forsaken them that seek thee.

March 23

There's no good thing the Lord will withhold from you. He gladly grant unto us our hearts' desires. He loves to please us and delights in our joy toward His goodness. He loves us so much that He's just waiting to hear our petition so He can perform it. He pours out His blessings upon us in abundance.

Word for the Day:

Psalm 36:7-9 (KJV)
   [9] How excellent is thy lovingkindness, O God! therefore the children of men put their trust under the shadow of thy wings. [8] They shall be abundantly satisfied with the fatness of thy house; and thou shalt make them drink of the river of thy pleasures. [9] For with thee is the fountain of life: in thy light shall we see light.

MARCH 24

I will make melody in my heart to God; I will lift my hands in adoration and bless Him with my lips. Today I was granted brand-new mercies, another opportunity to show forth your light and your word that speaks through my everyday walk. As I stay in your presence, I will be at peace and joyful. I desire to stay in your presence and don't want to be anywhere you're not. My soul longs for you.

WORD FOR THE DAY:

Psalm 89:15 (KJV)
[15] Blessed is the people that know the joyful sound: they shall walk, O Lord, in the light of thy countenance.

MARCH 25

Let's be grateful for all that God has done and will continue to do. It's so easy for us to complain about stuff. It takes a heart of thanksgiving to push past the negative thoughts and to cast down vain thoughts that are so totally unprosperous to the health of our souls and spirits. All that we have or ever hope to be is God's will for us. All through the day, let God know how much you love and appreciate Him, not just for what He has done for you but for who He is to you: a heart fixer and mind regulator, reminding you to be thankful for what you have. It's only then that you'll be blessed abundantly with more. He hates it when we complain, just as you would if your child complained about things that you have or have not done.

WORD FOR TODAY:

1 Corinthians 10:10 (KJV)
   Neither murmur ye, as some of them also murmured, and were destroyed of the destroyer.

MARCH 26

It's so easy to get anxious when we feel we are running out of time or that we need it quick, fast, and in a hurry, but when you really think about it, God knows and tells time for us. We need to pray and believe God will perform it in His time. He knows everything there is to know about you and more than you could ever know about yourself. We must rest in Him, knowing He will come through just in time.

WORD FOR TODAY:

Lamentations 3:24-25 (KJV)
   The Lord is my portion, saith my soul; therefore will I hope in him. [25] The Lord is good unto them that wait for him, to the soul that seeketh him.

MAY 27

I like living this kind of life, actually, I love living my life for Christ. Being used by Him is the most rewarding feeling in this world. You see, living for Him means fulfillment in every area of my life. My desire is to please Him, to show people that He is love and peace and that no matter what I face, I'm going to face it with joy because He is my salvation. He will see me through. Do not look on the things that are before you but look to Jesus who is the author and the finisher of your faith. He will never let you down. His face smiles down on me, and I shall forever bask in His goodness and rejoice in my everlasting salvation.

Isaiah 12:3 (KJV)
Therefore with joy shall ye draw water out of the wells of salvation.

Psalm 21:6 (KJV)
For thou hast made him most blessed for ever: thou hast made him exceeding glad with thy countenance.

MARCH 28

We must condition our minds to focus on God and His goodness so that we may stay in perfect peace. We can rest assured that, as we keep our focus on Him, our circumstances will diminish. We must put Him higher than any problems, not giving place to the enemy and His devices. God is far greater than anything, and it all works out in our favor every time.

WORD FOR TODAY:

Isaiah 26:3 (KJV)
Thou wilt keep him in perfect peace, whose mind is stayed on thee: because he trusteth in thee.

MARCH 29

Many things come up to distract you, taking your attention off the Lord. We must remember that everything happens for a reason, so in everything, we must give God praise and ask Him to teach us what is to be learned from the situation. There will always be seasons, some are more challenging than others, but it's important to realize that seasons change. We must accept the good as well as learn from the bad and know that all things will work out for our good. We must trust God who created the seasons and understand nothing just happens. He is the master of the universe and controls all that pertain to you. Every day, ask the Holy Spirit to guide you and trust Him to do just that.

Word for Today:

Ecclesiastes 3:1 (KJV)
> To every thing there is a season, and a time to every purpose under the heaven:

MARCH 30

As today starts, I commit my day and ways to the Lord. He will orchestrates the events of my day. I will trust Him as He unfold things before me. I will see with my spiritual eyes and hear with my spiritual ears. He has something great in store for me, so I wait with great expectancy.

WORD FOR TODAY:

Proverbs 3:5 (KJV)
> Trust in the Lord with all thine heart; and lean not unto thine own understanding.

MARCH 31

Today as everything seems to confuse, distract, and detain you, exhale and ask God to formulate your thoughts, your actions, and your speech. Of course, your insides are going haywire with all kinds of anxiousness, thinking of all that you have before you. However, that still, small voice speaks and says to calm down, be still, it's okay, and I'm with you. Even in this, I'm in control. There is divine purpose behind everything; stop and think about the plans you made without seeking His direction. Let God in and ask Him for His guidance. As you seek His counsel, things calm, and He gives you clarity to do His will. Any time you are confused, stop and ask God for help, and instantly, He does just that. You're not in this walk alone. My peace I give you.

WORD FOR TODAY:

Colossians 3:15 (KJV)
> And let the peace of God rule in your hearts, to the which also ye are called in one body; and be ye thankful.

TAKE AWAYS (NOTES)

APRIL

Isaiah 55:10 KJV - [10] For as the rain cometh down, and the snow from heaven, and returneth not thither, but watereth the earth, and maketh it bring forth and bud, that it may give seed to the sower, and bread to the eater:

APRIL 1

Everything is seemed to be designed to keep you away from God and communing with Him. The fellowship and closeness that God desires with us will mature your trust and understanding of Him so much so that the enemy tries to stunt your relationship with Him. Get to know Jesus for yourself; the more you know Him, the more you will want to know Him. If you draw nigh to God, He will draw nigh to you. Talk to Him; there can be no relationship without communication. No matter what it is, your joys, fears, your pains, even insecurities—just talk to Him about it, He will listen, and He will help you. He cares about everything related to you, He just wants you to feel or be close enough to Him to share it.

Word for Today:

1 Thessalonians 5:17 (KJV)
   Pray without ceasing.

April 2

Is there anything too hard for God? Can God do whatever you need? Yes He can and He will, if you only believe. God wants to be a show off; He wants to show you His infinite power by doing what no other can do. So when it's that ninth hour, trust God; when the doctors give up, trust God; when you don't know what to do, trust God; and when you've done all you can do, trust God. He already knows the outcome, so don't forget to include Him in all your decisions, He has the final and right word for the situation. He's so awesome. But you have got to be obedient to God's word and believe what He has said. Ask and believe is a very simple equation. Request + Faith = Answer

Word for Today:

Philippians 4:19 (KJV)
   But my God shall supply all your need according to his riches in glory by Christ Jesus.

2 Corinthians 4:17 (KJV)
   For our light affliction, which is but for a moment, worketh for us a far more exceeding and eternal weight of glory;

April 3

Our desire should be to be closer to God and in His presence. He's the person you should want to please at all times. Just think about a minute. He has the answer to every problem, every question, every hope, and every desire. He's the man—not your boss, nor children, and guess what, not even the banks or loan company is not as great as our God. God is our source, and we should be looking to Him and not man for everything. Whatever or whoever absorbs all your time and thoughts is your God. If all you think about is money or what you look like or your clothes, that's your God. If all you think about is your weight, it becomes your god. Spend time, a lot of time, with our Lord. He said if you draw nigh to Him, He will

draw nigh to you. So while you are trying to figure it out, God has it already worked out. He's just that type of God. Set your affections and desires on things eternal; that's what will last.

Word for Today:

Ephesians 3:20 (KJV)
> Now unto him that is able to do exceeding abundantly above all that we ask or think, according to the power that worketh in us,

2 Corinthians 4:18 (KJV)
> While we look not at the things which are seen, but at the things which are not seen: for the things which are

seen are temporal; but the things which are not seen are eternal.

April 4

To be more like Jesus is something we should all desire and seek after. After all we have His DNA, spiritually. We should put much effort in getting to know Him as we would in any physical or natural relationship. Spend quiet time alone with Him, allowing His sweet Spirit to minister to your soul. Even when your efforts yield short time spurts or little-to-no quality time, remember God sees and knows all. He knows your efforts, and they aren't fruitless. Make time for what's important — your Eternal Father, Savior, Lifeline, and Peacegiver. Don't take Him for granted simply because you know He's there; spend time talking, listening, loving, and thanking Him. He loves it.

Word for Today:

2 Chronicles 16:9 (KJV)
> For the eyes of the Lord run to and fro throughout the whole earth, to shew himself strong in the behalf of them whose heart is perfect toward him. Herein thou hast done foolishly: therefore from henceforth thou shalt have wars.

April 5

Many times we feel inadequate or undeserving of God's love when we are tempted. Not realizing, it's a normal function of the natural body to be tempted, even Paul said, "Oh wretched man that I am, who shall deliver me from the body of this death, when I want to do right, evil is always present." God's strength is made perfect in our weakness, so don't allow the enemy of our minds to make us feel bad for being tempted to do wrong; the sin is yielding to it. God has empowered us with His Holy Spirit, which will keep us from yielding. The thoughts and desires will come, but you can withstand them, tear down, plead the blood, and you will stand. The enemy who brings the warfare to your mind will have to go, and you will succeed in doing what is right and pleasing unto the Lord.

Word for Today:

2 Corinthians 4:7 (KJV)
   But we have this treasure in earthen vessels, that the excellency of the power may be of God, and not of us.

April 6

I'm learning in all things to be content and be always thankful. God knows what I need and will give me the desires of my heart. I thank God for where I've been, where He has brought me, and where He will lead me. I will keep my heart and my thankfulness at all times for all things and will not covet what others may have.

Word for Today:

Psalm 116:17 (KJV)
> I will offer to thee the sacrifice of thanksgiving, and will call upon the name of the Lord.

1 John 1:7 (KJV)
> But if we walk in the light, as he is in the light, we have fellowship one with another, and the blood of Jesus Christ his Son cleanseth us from all sin.

April 7

My God, early will I seek your face and ask your guidance throughout the day. I know things will come my way to distract me, to throw me off the course you have prepared for me. Guide my footsteps, Lord; may I forever follow your lead. You are my God, and I am your child, I shall forever be indebted to you for all that you have done and will continue to do in my life. My heart's desire is to be pleasing in your sight. I serve you alone.

Word for Today:

Psalm 27:8 (KJV)
> When thou saidst, Seek ye my face; my heart said unto thee, Thy face, Lord, will I seek.

APRIL 8

As I look out the window of the dawning of a brand new day, I see God's mercy and I feel His grace, not just for His children but for the world. Who could escape after neglecting so great of salvation. God is just in all that He does, it is man who has continued over and over again to reject Him.. If you take a look at nature itself, the trees lift its leafy branches in praise, the flowers are arrayed in beautiful colors and scents. Each day that God graces us with, we must give Him praise, glory and honor. Throughout the day we should make melody in our heart to Him, thanking Him for all He has done, what He is doing and what He will do in the future. We must talk with Him throughout the day, thanking Him for strength, courage and wisdom to make the right choices, to do the right things and to season our words with grace as we encounter challenges throughout our day.

WORD FOR TODAY:

Psalms 34:1 (KJV)
>[1} I will bless the Lord at all times, His praise shall continually be in my mouth. [2] My soul shall make her boast in the Lord: the humble shall hear thereof, and be glad. [3] O magnify the Lord with me, and let us exalt his name together.

APRIL 9

God put Himself into our very existence. How could we doubt that He wants our best as He has given us His best of everything — even life everlasting? We will never die, just as He will never die. What more could we ask for; nothing is worth being separated from our God. He is everything, He is more than the world, for we all know He created it as well.

WORD FOR TODAY:

Romans 8:38-39 (KJV)

> [39] For I am persuaded, that neither death, nor life, nor angels, nor principalities, nor powers, nor things present, nor things to come, [39] Nor height, nor depth, nor any other creature, shall be able to separate us from the love of God, which is in Christ Jesus our Lord.

APRIL 10

It's really funny how when things are going really well, we forget to pray and neglect to be thankful. I don't know if it's because we think that we are controlling things and taking care of business by staying on top of things. God is giving us the ability to keep it all together. We must put our trust in God, through the good and bad, through the hard times and easy times. God has His hands in everything that we do. Yes, we sometimes forget to include Him in our planning process and decision making. We get so caught up that we forget to remember who is really in control and has your life already planned, the One who sits high and looks low. It's never the right time to leave God out of the equation and trust in your own ability. Let's trust God through all things and with all things.

WORD FOR TODAY:

Jeremiah 17:7 (KJV)
[7] Blessed is the man that trusteth in the Lord, and whose hope the Lord is.

APRIL 11

When we think about the person we use to be, it should make us cringe and thankful at the same time. God looked beyond our mess and made it our message. He uses the things we've experienced to be a message of victory to others. It's only through His love and grace that He redeemed us from our mess. It's all about Him; we learn from the sin that we were in. A life without Christ is something we couldn't even conceive of once we receive Him. He gives us a solid and firm foundation of assurance in Him that there's no way of turning back.

WORD FOR TODAY:

Psalm 40:2 (KJV)
[2] He brought me up also out of an horrible pit, out of the miry clay, and set my feet upon a rock, and established my goings.

April 12

We always have choices either to believe God or not to believe Him. It takes experience to believe God in every situation. Therefore, we must weather the storm in order to produce the endurance we need for whatever battles we must face. We must trust God in all things for all things. He can and He will take care of us if we just believe. It's so much better than the alternative. Why not believe God and praise Him in advance for seeing you through, working things out for your good. Every day we must reinforce our trust in Him, tell Him you trust Him and love Him and watch things turn for your good.

Word for Today:

Psalm 31:14 (KJV)
[14]But I trusted in thee, O Lord: I said, Thou art my God.

April 13

I can do nothing apart from the vine that gives life to me spiritually. I am in Christ as Christ is in me. Out of love, respect and connection, I consult continuously with Him for all things. I honor Him as my Father by seeking Him all day long, even in the quiet moments that seems to be my time but actually is our quality time to commune. So in all things and at all times, I will seek to be in His presence where I am safe.

APRIL

WORD FOR TODAY:

John 15:5 (KJV)
> [15] I am the vine, ye are the branches: He that abideth in me, and I in him, the same bringeth forth much fruit: for without me ye can do nothing.

APRIL 14

Life is God because He is life; everything that lives has its being because of Him. We must thank God each day that we live for life now and everlasting life in the future. We must walk by faith and hope in the God of life and peace. Only then can we live life in its fullness with the blessing of life in the present and everlasting life that is to come because Jesus died, making it possible for us to live forever. Every living thing embraces His presence in their existence. Let us gratefully praise His life that runs through our spiritual veins.

WORD FOR TODAY:

Hebrews 6:19 (KJV)
> [19] Which hope we have as an anchor of the soul, both sure and stedfast, and which entereth into that within the veil.

APRIL 15

When things seems out of control and my spirit is weak, it is then when God will carry me and lead me to that place of peace. He is my refuge and my strength in times of weakness. He never leave me, nor will He forsake me. I will trust in Him, even when my feeble body and mind don't understand. I will trust that He knows what is best for me. He protects me from the evil hand of the enemy at all times, He carries me safely through troubles seen and unseen. I'm safe in His mighty arms. I have nothing and no one to fear.

Word for Today:

Psalm 61:2-4 (KJV)
> [2] From the end of the earth will I cry unto thee, when my heart is overwhelmed: lead me to the rock that is higher than I. [3] For thou hast been a shelter for me, and a strong tower from the enemy. [4] I will abide in thy tabernacle for ever: I will trust in the covert of thy wings. Selah.

April 16

In everything, give thanks. Accept each day with all its challenges and be thankful. God has full control; never complain, but ask God for guidance to learn what is to be learned.

Word for Today:

1 Thessalonians 5:18 (KJV)
> [18] In every thing give thanks: for this is the will of God in Christ Jesus concerning you.

APRIL 17

Many things come our way to distract us from our God, to take our mind off of Him and drive emotions that are contrary. They come to bring fear, worry, and defeat. But just remember that God is right there, so talk to Him and get in His presence; He will lead you safely through whatever the challenges are that you face. God is far greater than any circumstances that you may face, so remember to take it Him and leave it with Him. He cares and will take care of everything that concerns you.

WORD FOR TODAY:

Isaiah 41:10 (KJV)
> [10] Fear thou not; for I am with thee: be not dismayed; for I am thy God: I will strengthen thee; yea, I will help thee; yea, I will uphold thee with the right hand of my righteousness.

APRIL 18

Our life is in the Master's hand, nothing shall come against us and prevail. God takes really good care of us, and He has given us the power and authority to render evil helpless. We command evil tidings to leave; actually, we should command them to be silent. We are able to tread over poisonous vipers and not die. That means we can bind up the hand of the enemy in every situation in Jesus' name, and they have to cease.

Word for Today:

Psalm 112:7 (KJV)
   [7] He shall not be afraid of evil tidings: his heart is fixed, trusting in the Lord.

April 19

We so often feel undeserving or even inadequate of God's love and mercy that He liberally gives us twenty-four hours a day and seven days a week. There's nothing we have done or will do that will ever make us feel worthy enough. You are loved of God no matter what you do or don't do. He loves us unconditionally. So don't allow the enemy to plague you with guilt or lack, God knows you and accepts you for who you are, and that love makes you do better and be better automatically. Keep growing as you go through this journey of life, God loves you and always will.

Word for Today:

Jeremiah 31:3 (KJV)
   [3] The Lord hath appeared of old unto me, saying, Yea, I have loved thee with an everlasting love: therefore with lovingkindness have I drawn thee.

Isaiah 61:10 (KJV)
   [10] I will greatly rejoice in the Lord, my soul shall be joyful in my God; for he hath clothed me with the garments of salvation, he hath covered me with the robe

of righteousness, as a bridegroom decketh himself with ornaments, and as a bride adorneth herself with her jewels.

APRIL 20

Life can deal us a blow sometimes that it's incomprehensible; you just can't understand why. We start to allow all types of negative feelings to overtake us. Turn off whatever has you feeling depressed, sickness, scared, or lonely. Turn it off and turn to the word. Talk to the Lord, and let Him lift your burden and release the fear inside. Let it go so that you can live life to the fullest here on the earth and then everlasting glorious life eternally. God is with you, holding you by your right hand, so don't let go, don't give in, and never give out. He is the only solid foundation that you can trust to stand upon and having done all to stand, stand. There's nothing to fear; God is always near.

WORD FOR TODAY:

Deuteronomy 31:6 (KJV)
[6] Be strong and of a good courage, fear not, nor be afraid of them: for the Lord thy God, he it is that doth go with thee; he will not fail thee, nor forsake thee.

APRIL 21

God resists the proud but gives His grace to the humble. When we realize the sovereignty of God, it should give us a different perspective on life. His desire is for us to acknowledge Him and give Him honor in everything. Never taking credit for what you do for others. When people say that you are a blessing, it's okay to say thank you, but I give all the glory to God. In me (my flesh) dwells no good thing. It's only through His spirit that I am able to be a blessing.

Word for Today:

James 4:10
>[10] Humble yourselves in the sight of the Lord, and He will lift you up..

April 22

Everything is going down but the word of God. It's only the pure in heart who will see God. Therefore, we must cleanse our hearts from any wicked desires or thoughts. God knows our hearts, our thoughts, and our intensions, whether good or evil. He has made us free from any demonic evil force, but we must accept that freedom and turn away from any negative thoughts or feelings. Know God's word, what it says, and neglect not to do accordingly. Accept God, and you accept life everlasting.

Word for Today:

Proverbs 19:21 (KJV)
>There are many devices in a man's heart; nevertheless the counsel of the Lord, that shall stand.

APRIL 23

In all things and every situation, we must stay focused and not lose sight of our omnipotent God, who is everywhere and knows all things. Nothing takes Him by surprise, so don't let it take you by surprise and throw you off course. Stay in God's presence; He will surely give you direction. Talk to Him, pray about it, and trust Him to work all things out for your good. When you stay focused on Him, you will not slip and you will not fall. You will remain steadfast, and the enemy can't do you any harm. He will never leave you nor forsake you. He is there always, even throughout all eternity.

WORD FOR TODAY:

Psalm 141:8 (KJV)
>But mine eyes are unto thee, O God the Lord: in thee is my trust; leave not my soul destitute.

APRIL 24

There is no better way to live than in Christ. We can rest in knowing He is a present help when we are in need, and He's always there, encouraging us, loving us, and bringing us new mercies daily. He never ridicule or put us down, He's always there lifting us up, letting us know there's nothing we can do that will make Him not love us. There is no condemnation. Let us keep our mind on Him on spiritual everlasting things that shall never perish. In all things, we must rest in knowing,

God is there, so don't be anxious. Rest in His authority and love for you.

Word for Today:

Romans 8:1 (KJV)
> There is therefore now no condemnation to them which are in Christ Jesus, who walk not after the flesh, but after the Spirit.

April 25

We live in an ever-changing world. Our lives are forever changing, situations change, people come and go, and they love you one minute but not the next. The one thing that you can truly count on is God. His unchanging hands are ones that you can count on to hold you and keep you safe. Trust God's unchanging, unwavering hands and keep Him the focal point of your life. He will surely keep you in perfect peace.

Word for Today:

Psalm 102:27 (KJV)
> But thou art the same, and thy years shall have no end.

April 26

This too shall pass, whatever you are going through; it won't last always, and it will work out for your good. God is chief in command, and His thoughts of you are good. When things seems out of sync and you have no immediate solution, continue to look to God; it will work out for your good.

WORD FOR TODAY:

2 Corinthians 4:16-18 (KJV)
> For which cause we faint not; but though our outward man perish, yet the inward man is renewed day by day. [17] For our light affliction, which is but for a moment, worketh for us a far more exceeding and eternal weight of glory; [18] While we look not at the things which are seen, but at the things which are not seen: for the things which are seen are temporal; but the things which are not seen are eternal

APRIL 27

God wouldn't tell us to do the impossible. It appears that no one thinks that God intended them to be perfect or holy. God is just and true; if we couldn't do it, He wouldn't have commanded us to be holy or perfect. It's an excuse that enemy speaks to us to keep us bound and from walking in our calling. We can do all things by the power of Holy Spirit. Allow Him to make us perfect to the things we know to be perfect too. Allow Him to make us holy, just as He is holy. Our actions should be to please our holy and perfect God.

WORD FOR TODAY:

James 1:15

> But as He who called you is holy, you also be holy in all your conduct.

Matthew 5:48 KJV

> [48] Be ye therefore perfect, even as your Father which is in heaven is perfect.

APRIL 28

Jesus redeemed us by the blood that He shed at the cross. He paid the price for our freedom, He gave the ultimate sacrifice and declared no one took His life, but He gave it. He loved us so much that He died so that we can live eternally with Him.. We no longer have to offer the blood of animals, no longer do we have to go behind the veil, but we can come boldly before the throne to find grace in our time of need. God will forgive us for the sin we committed when we ask and turn to Him in faith.

WORD FOR THE DAY:

Ephesians 1:7

> In Him we have redemption through His blood, the forgiveness of sins, according to the riches of His grace.

April 29

Do you get excited when you read the word of God; are you in great anticipation of what He will speak to you? The word of God is nourishment for us, we simply cannot live without it. It is our life source to sustain a healthy spiritual life. As we read and meditate on it, our relationship with Him grows and mature in such a way that we have withdrawals if we don't read and spend time with Him daily. We should light up when it's time to relate with God.

Word for Today:

Proverbs 7:2
> [2] Keep my commands and live, and my law as the apple of your eye.

April 30

Each day brings about new experiences, new challenges, or maybe even a familiar challenge that we need to handle a new way. No matter what a day brings, we can trust that God is in it, and He will lift you up, He will sustain you by His strength. We fall into different temptations. It happens unintentionally; no one falls intentionally as though it's a mistake you couldn't prevent. So we must count it joy because the fall made us realize we are imperfect creatures working toward perfection. It allows us to count and depend more on God's strength than our own. That's the reason we must walk in the spirit. So we can see with our spiritual eyes and not so much as the natural naked eye because we just might miss something.

Word for Today:

James 1:2 (KN)
> My brethren, count it all joy when ye fall into divers temptations.

TAKE AWAYS (NOTES)

MAY

*Isaiah 43:19 KJV - **[19]** Behold, I will do a new thing; now it shall spring forth; shall ye not know it? I will even make a way in the wilderness, and rivers in the desert.*

MAY 1

Live for today, now is the appointed time. To live for today and worry about nothing is God's will for you. Today is the Lord's day, and He has commissioned it to bring forth all the challenges that He knew you could handle. Don't worry; be happy.

WORD FOR TODAY:

Luke 12:25–26 (KJV)
 And which of you with taking thought can add to his stature one cubit? [26] If ye then be not able to do that thing which is least, why take ye thought for the rest?

MAY 2

It's so easy to get caught up into what man thinks of us or even what they do, taking us somewhere we should not be. We should focus on pleasing God, and He will work through you to get to man what they need. We can't please God and please man, too. It's impossible to have two guides. We must depend solely on the one true guide, the Holy Spirit. There is life and peace in Him.

Word for Today:

Proverbs 29:25 (KJV)
> The fear of man bringeth a snare: but whoso putteth his trust in the Lord shall be safe.

May 3

It would seem this term is an oxymoron but many of us are guilty of just that. We worry but our Master says pray. We try and make sense out of things, when our Master says, "Just trust me." We complain about what we don't have when our Master says, "I will supply all of your needs." I could go on and on with endless examples of how we try and serve two masters, but that's what makes things hard for us to depend absolutely on the supernatural power of our Lord God. We must let go, and let God. We must not worry but be happy. If we say that we are His, then let's believe the word and live by the word and have everlasting life, free of worry and strain. Letting go gets us blessings and all God has in store for us. He is our first and only true love, for in Him is truth and righteousness.

Word for Today:

Matthew 6:24 (KJV)
> No man can serve two masters: for either he will hate the one, and love the other; or else he will hold to the one, and despise the other. Ye cannot serve God and mammon.

Revelation 2:4 (KJV)
> Nevertheless I have somewhat against thee, because thou hast left thy first love.

Ephesians 3:16 (KJV)
> That he would grant you, according to the riches of his glory, to be strengthened with might by his Spirit in the inner man;

Ephesians 3:17 (KJV)
> That Christ may dwell in your hearts by faith; that ye, being rooted and grounded in love.

Psalm 16:11 (KJV)
> Thou wilt shew me the path of life: in thy presence is fullness of joy; at thy right hand there are pleasures for evermore.

May 4

Though we haven't seen God, we love Him. We love Him intimately for who He is to us. Just for looking into the future and

SCENT OF HEAVEN

bringing us forth unto His glory and for His honor, we love Him. It's not because we loved Him first, but He first loved us and chose us for such a time as this. This exact moment in time was ordained by the unseeded, much-loved God. We have continuous joy in that no matter what comes our way, He is that unseen force that constantly protects and keeps from danger seen and unseen, as well as pouring out tremendous blessings and brand-new mercies each and every day.

WORD FOR TODAY:

1 Peter 1:8 (KJV)
>Whom having not seen, ye love; in whom, though now ye see him not, yet believing, ye rejoice with joy unspeakable and full of glory:

MAY 5

What a mighty God we serve! He deserve more praises than we are giving Him. He's a God who can do anything but fail. Failure isn't an option; it's not even in His vocabulary. Ask what you will, and it shall be given unto you. Then began to give Him the praise.

WORD FOR TODAY:

Psalm 95:2 (KJV)
>Let us come before his presence with thanksgiving, and make a joyful noise unto him with psalms.

May 6

It's so easy to get distracted. There are so many things to take our minds off of God and His will for our lives. We allow things that are menial and temporal to consistently throw us off course. See God in all things and ask for guidance. Look for the spiritual and allow the Holy Spirit to manifest and bring clarity to all your circumstances. When you bring God in your circumstances, you walk in the Spirit, knowing these things are only temporary and will soon pass. Take the time to spend time with the Father of time, and then you will how to divide time.

Word for Today:

Isaiah 26:3 (KJV)
> Thou wilt keep him in perfect peace, whose mind is stayed on thee: because he trusteth in thee.

2 Corinthians 4:18 (KJV)
> While we look not at the things which are seen, but at the things which are not seen: for the things which are seen are temporal; but the things which are not seen are eternal.

May 7

I shall not fret what today or any day may bring, I trust God. My life is in Him, my every situation is in Him. There's no harm that can overtake me that He doesn't know about, there's no valley too deep for me because He knows how much I can handle, nor is there a mountain too high for me because He knows how high I can climb. Even if I should stumble He already knew I'd get up and learn the lesson. So why should I fear or be ashamed, God takes me through every challenge I face. As a matter of fact He had a hand in it.

Word of the Day:

Genesis 50:20 (KJV)
> But as for you, ye thought evil against me; but God meant it unto good, to bring to pass, as it is this day, to save much people alive.

May 8

Know that tribulations has to come, but the Lord delivers us out of them all. He will hold us by His right and walk us safely through. These things are temporal, but Heaven is eternal. You have an eternity to live free of problems, so just look at problems as an exercise in faith to help you through this life's journey. With Jesus you can make it. No matter what comes or who goes, your life is wrapped up, tied up, and tangled up in Jesus. You can make it through. It's only temporary.

WORD FOR TODAY:

John 16:33 (KJV)
> These things I have spoken unto you, that in me ye might have peace. In the world ye shall have tribulation: but be of good cheer; I have overcome the world.

MAY 9

Don't fear man who can only destroy the body, but fear God who can destroy both body and soul in hell. It's so crazy how the enemy tries to outsmart us and make us think that He has power. We have not only power but authority; he has power but no authority over us. When you speak God's word, he trembles with fear. Resist the enemy and he will flee. Don't ever think he has the rule over you. If it is God's will for you to perish, you will perish and obtain eternity, so it's still a win-win situation. For me to live is Christ and to die is to gain eternal life.

WORD FOR TODAY:

2 Corinthians 1:8–9 (KJV)
> For we would not, brethren, have you ignorant of our trouble which came to us in Asia, that we were pressed out of measure, above strength, insomuch that we despaired even of life: [9] But we had the sentence of death in ourselves, that we should not trust in ourselves, but in God which raiseth the dead:

May 10

In my season of trouble, the Lord shall keep me in perfect peace. I know my light afflictions are but for a moment and there's a blessing in every lesson; this is just a test. God will see me through the difficult times in my life and guide me safely through. No matter what comes my way, I will trust in the redeeming blood of Jesus. I will speak life in every situation, knowing that I'm more than a conqueror through Him who nailed all problems, sickness, and disease to the cross, I just have to believe and not complain. Embrace each situation as an opportunity to learn.

Word for Today:

John 15:5 (KJV)
I am the vine, ye are the branches: He that abideth in me, and I in him, the same bringeth forth much fruit: for without me ye can do nothing.

May 11

When we put our trust in God and no one else, things work out. God will not have anything or anyone else before Him. He will move Heaven and Earth to fulfill His purpose in us, so we must trust that He will supply *all* of our needs. We shall not want for anything. If we are suffering lack in any area of our lives we best check ourselves; it's never God.

WORD FOR TODAY:

Philippians 4:6 (KJV)
> Be careful for nothing; but in every thing by prayer and supplication with thanksgiving let your requests be made known unto God.

MAY 12

Growing in God changes our attitude toward evil. We no longer desire to sin, and if we do sin, it's not planned. The sinner sins because that's who he is and what he does. The believer sins unintentionally and feels conviction to repent; it's no longer natural for us. We fear God and never want to disappoint Him by evil. As a matter of fact, we hate sin as much as He does.

WORD FOR TODAY:

Proverbs 8:13
> "The fear of the LORD is to hate evil.."

MAY 13

I will not be disturbed by unwanted or unpleasant circumstances, knowing that I have but to trust God, even in the midst of the circumstance. I know there's a blessing in every lesson if I just look to Jesus for the answers and not trust in myself.

Word for Today:

1 Peter 5:6-7 (KJV)
> Humble yourselves therefore under the mighty hand of God, that he may exalt you in due time: [7] Casting all your care upon him; for he careth for you.

May 14

God loves a pure heart—one who seeks to please Him, who does what is right in the sight of God and toward his neighbor. Not only will we see God in heaven, but we see Him in our everyday life. We are able to see God in the hearts of His people here in the earth and in keeping our land safe.

Word for Today:

Matthew 5:8 KJV
> [8] Blessed are the pure in heart: for they shall see God.

May 15

It's so easy to fall prey to the devices of the enemy. He's constantly on the job of distracting, enticing, manipulating, and accusing the children of God. We have to be on our job as God's children, being wise as serpents and harmless as doves. It's our nature not to react to negativity; it's not the first thing we think about when someone is ugly toward us. It becomes a second thought to respond back negatively. Our first instincts as Christians now should be pleasant. Once you think about their actions, you think man, I should have said something back ugly. Christ is in you now, and we react differently when we walk in the spirit. It's an afterthought to be ugly that the enemy puts there, making you feel weak or like a martyr. Rebuke him and keep it moving.

WORD FOR TODAY:

Revelation 12:10 (KJV)
> And I heard a loud voice saying in heaven, Now is come salvation, and strength, and the kingdom of our God, and the power of his Christ: for the accuser of our brethren is cast down, which accused them before our God day and night.

Ephesians 6:6-7 (KJV)
> Not with eye service, as men pleasers; but

MAY 16

There are so many things that cloud our judgment and take us away from where God would have us. We are constantly making plans and moving in directions that we never even brought the Lord into, nor did we ask for direction. We must trust in the Lord with all of our hearts, knowing that He knows what we don't. We should seek guidance and counsel throughout the day, and only then can we honestly say that we are walking in the Spirit. Trust not in yourselves because you have no control over your life; only God does.

Word for Today:

Proverbs 19:21 (KJV)
> There are many devices in a man's heart; nevertheless the counsel of the Lord, that shall stand.

May 17

We serve a God of more than enough, who has everything. He can do anything but fail. There's nothing too hard for Him, He will never fall short of His word. Your request is but a prayer of faith away. If you believe, then receive; it is already established in Heaven, if you only believe.

Word for Today:

Philippians 4:19 (KJV)
> But my God shall supply all your need according to his riches in glory by Christ Jesus.

May 18

If we are faith walkers, why do we get afraid when we see Goliath? God loves it when we live by faith in Him, knowing that we cannot be moved by what is in front of us and we are only moved by what we believe God is doing. He is working it out for our good.

WORD FOR TODAY:

2 Corinthians 5:7 (KJV)
   For we walk by faith, not by sight.

MAY 19

I will consciously include the Lord in the day that He mercifully gave me. He will lead, guide, and direct my feet along the path He has already established for me. I shall not fear but trust in God with all my heart from here to eternity.

WORD FOR TODAY:

1 Corinthians 13:12 (KJV)
   For now we see through a glass, darkly; but then face to face: now I know in part; but then shall I know even as also I am known.

WORD FOR TODAY:

1 Corinthians 13:12 (KJV)
   For now we see through a glass, darkly; but then face to face: now I know in part; but then shall I know even as also I am known.

MAY 20

One day in heaven we will pay for everything we endured on the earth. God has created a place for us to dwell in happiness and bliss for all eternity. We will not remember the pains and sorrow of our time on earth, for God Himself shall wipe it from our memory. He loves us that much; He doesn't even want us to remember the former things.

WORD FOR TODAY:

Revelation 7:17
    God will wipe every tear from their eyes.

MAY 21

If God is for us, He is all you need. You should not suffer lack for anything. We can and will conquer anything that seems to come against us through His power. We have access to the very best there is; we have God, Jesus, and the Holy Spirit dwelling on the inside. We are empowered to get what we need. God is the very source of everything, and He will move heaven and earth to fulfill His will. He cannot fall short on nothing that He has said. Proclaim and stand on the word of God, which is able to keep us in all things.

WORD FOR TODAY:

Romans 8:31-32 (KJV)
    What shall we then say to these things? If God be for us, who can be against us? [32] He that spared not his own Son, but delivered him up for us all, how shall he not with him also freely give us all things?

May 22

We don't have to pretend to be holy; we are holy. We don't have to prove to anyone our salvation. God made our salvation sure through His son Jesus. The only reason people want to be heard and seen is because the want the glory, not God.

Word for Today:

Matthew 6:5 KJV
> [5] And when thou prayest, thou shalt not be as the hypocrites are: for they love to pray standing in the synagogues and in the corners of the streets, that they may be seen of men. Verily I say unto you, They have their reward.

May 23

God wants all of you, no matter who you are, what you possess, or what your title is. God is to be honored and glorified. He is the one who gives you all things, and when we are of haughty spirit, He will take it away. We must always submit to the higher authority in Christ Jesus and the spiritual covering that He gives us in the earth.

Word for Today:

Matthew 8:9 KJV
> [9] For I am a man under authority, having soldiers under me: and I say to this man, Go, and he goeth; and

SCENT OF HEAVEN

to another, Come, and he cometh; and to my servant, Do this, and he doeth it.

May 24

The most comfortable place to be is with the Lord, no matter what is going on in my life, I can find peace in His presence. There's no place more serene, peaceful, and joyous at the same time. This gives nourishment to my spirit and soul, it revitalizes my physical being. In His presence is all the answers of life in the present and all eternity.

Word for Today:

Genesis 3:8 (KJV)
And they heard the voice of the Lord God walking in the garden in the cool of the day: and Adam and his wife hid themselves from the presence of the Lord God amongst the trees of the garden.

May 25

Each day comes with various challenges, and we have to make the tough decisions. However, the good news is that we don't have to make them alone. The Holy Spirit is right there to help us. He's patiently awaiting us to acknowledge Him and include Him in our decision making. We can seek guidance, direction from Him. He is all knowing, so there's no battle too strong or decision too hard when you allow God to direct you.

WORD FOR TODAY:

Zephaniah 3:17 (KJV)
> The Lord thy God in the midst of thee is mighty; he will save, he will rejoice over thee with joy; he will rest in his love, he will joy over thee with singing.

MAY 26

There's a time and a season for everything: a time to laugh and a time to mourn—such is life. God will comfort us when we need comforting, He will never leave us uncovered to be buried in the sand of misery. He wants us to rejoice and be exceedingly glad. We get a moment to mourn and weep for a night season, but our joy comes in the morning with each brand-new day of mercies.

WORD FOR TODAY:

Matthew 5:4 KJV
> [4] Blessed are they that mourn: for they shall be comforted.

MAY 27

Just as the flowers need the rain, we need the Lord. Each day we awake and do those things necessary such as wash, clothe ourselves, and eat. In just the same way, we need to read His word and communicate with God daily for our spiritual nourishment and cleansing. It's not enough to do one and

SCENT OF HEAVEN

not the other; we need to put Him on and keep Him on and refresh often.

WORD FOR TODAY:

Psalm 27:8 (KJV)
> When thou saidst, Seek ye my face; my heart said unto thee, Thy face, Lord, will I seek.

Romans 13:14 (KJV)
> But put ye on the Lord Jesus Christ, and make not provision for the flesh, to fulfil the lusts thereof.

MAY 28

All hell could break lose and confusion surround you, but we know when we enter into the room or situation, the climate must change. The atmosphere must be conducive to our spirit, which is peaceable. When light comes, darkness has to go, because they can no coexist. The same holds true with confusion and discord; they can't coexist with peace. We have the peace of God resonating within us, and the situation has to change.

WORD OF THE DAY:

Matthew 5:9 KJV
> [9] Blessed are the peacemakers: for they shall be called the children of God.

May 29

I will embrace each day with the Lord, nothing can separate me from Him. He came to ensure that I'm never alone and that I might live free from sin. No matter what comes my way, I will endure with Christ; nothing is impossible for me.

Word for Today:

Colossians 2:6–7 (KJV)
> As ye have therefore received Christ Jesus the Lord, so walk ye in him: [7] Rooted and built up in him, and stablished in the faith, as ye have been taught, abounding therein with thanksgiving.

May 30

I want to know God's way and the way He thinks. My desire is to have the mind of Christ, His very essence radiating through me, a living, lively testimony of Him.

Word for Today:

Psalm 119:27 (KJV)
> Make me to understand the way of thy precepts: so shall I talk of thy wondrous works.

May 31

Knowing God is to know peace. In knowing God, you get acquainted with His very being. You come to understand that it is in and through Him that we live, move, and have our being. Life takes on a new and deeper meaning, realizing it's not in your control, but God is. Therefore, we have peace in Him, knowing everything will work out for our good. He is our Father, and there's no good thing He will withhold from His obedient children.

Word for Today:

Job 22:21 (KJV)
> Acquaint now thyself with him, and be at peace: thereby good shall come unto thee.

TAKE AWAYS (NOTES)

JUNE

Proverbs 1:8 KJV - [8] My son, hear the instruction of thy father, and forsake not the law of thy mother.

JUNE 1

What more can we ask for? He has given us everything; we just won't reach out and take it. We must trust that every word is true; if it's in God's word, we can count on it, live by it, and be comforted. No matter what a day brings, God is right there to guide us safely through. He will never leave us unprotected or alone.

WORD FOR TODAY:

Psalm 18:30 (KJV)
As for God, his way is perfect: the word of the Lord is tried: he is a buckler to all those that trust in him.

JUNE 2

We are adopted in the beloved, children of almighty God. He didn't keep anything back from us; we don't lack in any area of this life or the life to come. When He comes, we shall see Him face to face, and we shall be like Him, perfect in every way.

Word for Today:

1 John 3:2 (KJV)
> Beloved, now are we the sons of God, and it doth not yet appear what we shall be: but we know that, when he shall appear, we shall be like him; for we shall see him as he is.

June 3

Word for Today:

2 Thessalonians 3:16 (KJV)
> Now the Lord of peace himself give you peace always by all means. The Lord be with you all.

June 4

Word for Today:

Isaiah 26:3 (KJV)
> Thou wilt keep him in perfect peace, whose mind is stayed on thee: because he trusteth in thee.

JUNE 5

When we focus our attention on God and all the goodness He shows toward us in providing for all of our needs, we can do anything He calls us to do. We cannot do anything in and of ourselves; everything is through God. It is He who gives us the skills and intellect to reach goals and succeed in life. It's not you; you can't take credit for your life or anything that you've accomplished, or you risk making yourself a god. Our God is a jealous God and will not have any other before Him. He will not tolerate anyone taking credit for the things that He has done. Take no delight in yourself, but delight in God, the creator of all things.

WORD FOR TODAY:

Exodus 20:3 (KJV)
   Thou shalt have no other Gods before me.

Psalm 37:4 (KJV)
   Delight thyself also in the Lord; and he shall give thee the desires of thine heart.

JUNE 6

We must trust in God's strength; ours will fail us every time. When we seek His face daily, He will instruct us and guide us through every decision. We must see God in all things, thereby being in total dependence on Him and not ourselves. When we lose sight on Him and think it's about us, we fail miserably every time.

The world declares His glory and majesty, as the sun rises and the moon shines, and flowers bloom and the trees wave in praise. Surely I stand amazed to see the goodness of God in this life.

Word for the Day:

Psalm 105:4 (KJV)
   Seek the Lord, and his strength: seek his face evermore.

Psalm 19:1-2 (KJV)
   The heavens declare the glory of God; and the firmament sheweth his handywork. [2] Day unto day uttereth speech, and night unto night sheweth knowledge.

June 7

To worry or to pray — that is the question. I have found the answer. Worry about nothing and pray about everything. God knows what you need, and there's no good thing He will withhold from us who love and obey His word. As long as you stand on God's word, you cannot fall.

Lord, thank you for giving me peace and calmness in you to change the things that I can change, the courage to accept the things I can't change, and thank you for giving me wisdom to know the difference.

JUNE

Luke 12:22–31 (KJV)

And he said unto his disciples, Therefore I say unto you, Take no thought for your life, what ye shall eat; neither for the body, what ye shall put on. [23] The life is more than meat, and the body is more than raiment. [24] Consider the ravens: for they neither sow nor reap; which neither have storehouse nor barn; and God feedeth them: how much more are ye better than the fowls? [25] And which of you with taking thought can add to his stature one cubit? [26] If ye then be not able to do that thing which is least, why take ye thought for the rest? [27] Consider the lilies how they grow: they toil not, they spin not; and yet I say unto you, that Solomon in all his glory was not arrayed like one of these. [28] If then God so clothe the grass, which is to day in the field, and to morrow is cast into the oven; how much more will he clothe you, O ye of little faith? [29] And seek not ye what ye shall eat, or what ye shall drink, neither be ye of doubtful mind. [30] For all these things do the nations of the world seek after: and your Father knoweth that ye have need of these things. [31] But rather seek ye the kingdom of God; and all these things shall be added unto you.

John 16:33 (KJV)

These things I have spoken unto you, that in me ye might have peace. In the world ye shall have tribulation: but be of good cheer; I have overcome the world.

June 8

In a world so full of darkness and hopelessness, we are that beacon of light. We are God's workmanship and the world sees Him through our light. We are the light of the world as He is the light, and we live life through Him. We must show the people that God is God and there is no other God. The world in all its creation shows forth His glory: every star in the sky, every silver lining, the flowers and trees, both heaven above and the earth beneath and everything that dwells therein is His work of art. We are His works of art. God has taken our brokenness to show forth His majesty as He perfectly mends the pieces of our life.

He is the vine, and we are the branches. Our life is through the vine. In Him we live, move, and have our being. We must live our lives true to Him, showing the world His love and majesty through the life that we live in Him.

Father God of the Universe, God that created me perfect in you. I give me to you, I belong to you whole heartedly, aside from you I'm dead, I no longer exist. You are my life line, in you, I live, move, and have my being. I trust you with all of me and all the people who are surrounding you. I will ask you and believe that it shall be given. There is no good thing you will withhold from me. I love you, Lord, and know that your will is what's best for me. Though I may not understand the circumstances of this life, I trust you and will listen to your voice as you lead, guide, and direct me into all truth. In Jesus' name, through the power of the anointed Holy Ghost, I pray. Amen.

Psalm 19:1-2 (KJV)

The heavens declare the glory of God; and the firmament sheweth his handywork. [2] Day unto day uttereth speech, and night unto night sheweth knowledge.

June 9

It's so easy to see God in all things that surround us; the beauty and wonder of the elements proclaim His majestic power. He never cease to amaze me with His creativeness. Creation itself is a wonder of wonders. Everything is so intricately woven together to bring about His perfection. He laid the foundation and called everything into being. Where there was darkness, He created light, even in our lives. We were in a dark place without life, and He spoke life and we became beautiful spiritual beings. After He created the world, His workmanship, He declared it was good. So when you look in the mirror, you should see God.

Psalm 104:5 (KJV)
  Who laid the foundations of the earth, that it should not
  be removed for ever.

June 10

We have a tendency as humans to thank God when things are swell and well, but we neglect to thank Him during times of struggle, not remembering that God has hold of your hand and will bring you safely through the tough times. The tough times

SCENT OF HEAVEN

are for your breaking and making; the good times are rewards at the end of the challenge. There's a blessing in every lesson, so learn the lesson and receive your blessing. Wait on the Lord, and He will strengthen your soul as you journey through.

Word for Today:

1 Thessalonians 5:18 (KJV)
In every thing give thanks: for this is the will of God in Christ Jesus concerning you.

June 11

It's amazing how the very thing that the enemy try to use to destroy us, God uses to bring us closer to Him. When we worry, it brings us to our knees because there's no place else to turn. It allows a closer more intimate relationship with the Father. However, once we pray, we must believe that God has it and will work on our behalf. At some point, we must trust God to do what we in our human state cannot. Don't be afraid to let it go and let God have it.

Word for Today:

Isaiah 12:2 KJV
[2] Behold, God is my salvation; I will trust, and not be afraid: for the Lord Jehovah is my strength and my song; he also is become my salvation.

June 12

Every morning I awake and every breath I take is unto the Lord. It is He who gave us life, and we must live to give praise unto Him. Throughout the day, bless Him and do not complain, God brought you to it; surely He can and will bring you through it. See God in everything, see opportunity to show forth His goodness unto a lost and dying world. Even when the day looks dim, find light in Him by changing your focus from the dim circumstances to focusing on *God*, for in Him is light.

Word for Today:

1 Corinthians 10:10 KJV
> [10] Neither murmur ye, as some of them also murmured, and were destroyed of the destroyer.

June 13

It's so amazing how you can feel the joy of the Lord when all around you is in chaos. God knew we needed Him; to know Him is to know the fullness of His joy. Happiness is a fleeting emotion, but His joy is everlasting. He has given us the in dwelling of His Holy Spirit so that we can live life to the fullness, without reservation, guilt, or condemnation. He knows exactly what we need to live now, and He gives it to us liberally without fail.

Word for Today:

Galatians 5:22-23 KJV

[22] But the fruit of the Spirit is love, joy, peace, longsuffering, gentleness, goodness, faith,

June 14

Before the foundation of the world, God knew you. He knew everything there was to know, from your end to the beginning. He knew your failures and successes, He knew the pain and sufferings, He even knew you would sin and mess up time and time again, but He created you nonetheless. Why, just like a great Father, He loves you through the mess and make you His messenger. So no matter what you've done or will do, God loves you and will never turn His back on His child. Even when we turn away from Him, He waits with open arms to receive you. He will never hold your sins against you. After all, Jesus has already paid the price.

Word for Today:

Jeremiah 31:3 KJV

[3] The Lord hath appeared of old unto me, saying, Yea, I have loved thee with an everlasting love: therefore with lovingkindness have I drawn thee.

June 15

You are so beautiful in the eyes of our Father. So often, our vision gets distorted as we view ourselves with condemnation and unworthiness. We must learn to see ourselves as God sees us—fearfully and wonderfully made in His image. We can't allow the negativity of life to cause us to criticize our Father's creation. He has created us as it has pleased Him, not as it has pleased you. If you are good and beautiful enough for God, that's all that really matters. So accept all of God's creation: accept you, be ok with you, and be joyful about you, for you are the apple of His eye. He has chosen you and has clothed you with salvation, beauty, and righteousness. He has given us all that we need to presentable in His sight.

Word for Today:

Isaiah 61:10 KJV
> [10] I will greatly rejoice in the Lord, my soul shall be joyful in my God; for he hath clothed me with the garments of salvation, he hath covered me with the robe of righteousness, as a bridegroom decketh himself with ornaments, and as a bride adorneth herself with her jewels.

June 16

I am who God says that I am, who He created me to be, I am His workmanship. I'm not good in and of myself; only through God will I boast and honor. He is Lord of my life, and His way is prosperous. Therefore, I am prosperous and will continually keep His goodness before me.

WORD FOR TODAY:

Ephesians 2:10 KJV

> [10] For we are his workmanship, created in Christ Jesus unto good works, which God hath before ordained that we should walk in them.

JUNE 17

Human tendency is to long to be accepted, approved, affirmed, and applauded for what we do or for who we are. I went through a season of feeling rejected because I felt that I was not acknowledged or appreciated for anything that I did. God softly spoke to me (once I listened) and said, "My child, if you're expecting it from man, then don't expect it from me." Wow, how liberating was that for me. It freed me from people and their opinions. Let's not be concerned about what man thinks about us but what our Father knows about us, and He will reward us beyond what our natural mind can conceive. One day in God's kingdom will pay for everything you endured, and the extra bonus is that He will reward us for eternity.

Psalm 62:5 (KJV)

> My soul, wait thou only upon God; for my expectation is from him.

June 18

Many have been called, but few are chosen. I'm forever indebted and grateful to God for choosing me. You see, I only answered the call, but He chose me from the foundation of the world to lead a Christless world to Christ. I was accepted in the beloved way before I answered the call of God. He chose me to spend eternity with him. He loved me just that much. If you are filled with His Holy Spirit, you too are chosen, and none can take you away from Him. We aren't holy because of anything that we have done; we are holy because He is holy and His seed is in us, His DNA runs through our spiritual veins, which will last forever. We are forever filled, sealed, and holy.

Word for Today:

Ephesians 1:4 KJV
[4] According as he hath chosen us in him before the foundation of the world, that we should be holy and without blame before him in love:

June 19

I will bless the Lord at all times; His praise shall continuously be in my mouth. I am eternally grateful to God for not just calling but choosing me. Aren't you? What a blessing to know that every part of me, every part of you, from the inside out, belongs to God. Carefully we must possess our vessels while on loan to us. Be sure to thank God for good health and strength.

Be open to His guidance on what is best for His temple. We must acknowledge the fact that He gave us life. He entrusted us with His vessel and we *must* do what's right and pleasing unto Him, not what is pleasing and right to us. Obey His word and present yourself as a living sacrifice, holy and acceptable in His sight. Be mindful always of how you treat God's body. To neglect or mistreat it is to neglect and mistreat Him.

WORD FOR TODAY:

1 Corinthians 6:19-20 KJV
> [19] What? know ye not that your body is the temple of the Holy Ghost which is in you, which ye have of God, and ye are not your own? [20] For ye are bought with a price: therefore glorify God in your body, and in your spirit, which are God's.

JUNE 20

There are miracles each and every day we awake to a new sunrise and lie down to a new moon, stars, and elements. I see God throughout the day, performing miracles, giving signs, and keeping us in wonderment and amazement in all His glorious craftiness. When I seek Him, I get an immediate response — that's God. When I look at me and the changes that He has made in my life, in the life of my loved ones and others, I'm in complete awe of our God. A fool has said in his heart there is no God. Shame on them. Having eyes, they cannot see; neither having ears can they hear the marvelous words He speaks. God loves us so much, what more can I ask?

Word for Today:

Psalm 8:1–4 KJV

> [1] O Lord our Lord, how excellent is thy name in all the earth! who hast set thy glory above the heavens. [2] Out of the mouth of babes and sucklings hast thou ordained strength because of thine enemies, that thou mightest still the enemy and the avenger. [3] When I consider thy heavens, the work of thy fingers, the moon and the stars, which thou hast ordained; [4] What is man, that thou art mindful of him? and the son of man, that thou visitest him?

June 21

We are a time-conscious people; it's as though time controls us, instead of us being in control of time. God gave us time, and He wants us to use it wisely, which includes making Him, the Father of time, a priority and giving back to Him what He has so graciously given unto us. We must be apt to set time aside for communing with Him in unrushed, leisure time, where we can really relate and develop our relationship, always going deeper and closer. You see, the deeper and closer you get to God, the less the enemy will be able to use you. You grow confident in your relationship with Christ, and nothing or nobody can separate you from God.

Word for Today:

Micah 7:7 KJV

[7] Therefore I will look unto the Lord; I will wait for the God of my salvation: my God will hear me.

June 22

We as children of God must wear charity as a coat. Put it on and keep it on daily so that it covers you, protects you, and keeps you safe and warm. God is love, and because we are in Him as He dwells within us, we must show forth His love for all people. Yes, this includes your enemies. We must realize that love covers a multitude of sin. We must see man as God sees them: all souls are precious to Him. When we realize it is God who orchestrates the events in our lives and that He has empowered you with the ability to handle any situation, nothing just happens. Simply ask God to help you to understand the lesson that is being taught and pass the test so that you can go to the next level. Remember we wrestle not against flesh and blood, but against spiritual attacks. So keep on the whole armor of God, so you cannot only just fight but win.

Word of the Day:

1 Peter 4:8 (KJV)

And above all things have fervent charity among yourselves: for charity shall cover the multitude of sins.

JUNE 23

Love, such a small four-letter word, yet us so huge in meaning, which is demonstrated by our actions. When we give love, we are then able to receive love, not in the conditional way that the unbeliever loves, but the agape love that God demonstrates. We understand that love is what will draw the unbeliever, love is what will sustain relationships, love was from the beginning, and it will never fail. There's no need to fear anything or anybody when you truly show love. There's an old adage that says, "Love is what love does." If love isn't reciprocated, that is not on you, and you can't beat yourself up about that or fear that you can't go on. You can and you will; God gives you the strength to keep going, keep loving, and to be loved by those who matter.

WORD FOR TODAY:

1 John 4:18 (KJV)
> There is no fear in love; but perfect love casteth out fear: because fear hath torment. He that feareth is not made perfect in love.

JUNE 24

We should put our trust only in God and expect things to happen, changing only because of Him. When we trust in others, we are prone to disappointment. Yes, we should desire for people to keep their word and honor what they say, but God uses people. He moves through people. You never know what God is up to, but we know He only works for our best interest. Whatever happens, it is for our good.

WORD FOR TODAY:

Psalm 62:5-6 KJV
> [5] My soul, wait thou only upon God; for my expectation is from him. [6] He only is my rock and my salvation: he is my defence; I shall not be moved.

JUNE 25

You knew my ending from the beginning, Lord. You predestined me for your Kingdom. Before I was conceived in my mother's womb, you had established my life. Though you knew that I would stray from your truth, you loved me anyway and prepared a way for my safe return to you.

From a child I knew your holy word but didn't really know it for myself until I answered the call to your true salvation. You empowered me with strength to endure the hard times and the pleasure of sin that tried to reign in my flesh. You knew I needed you in order that I may remain in your royal court.

I thank you, Lord, for looking beyond my faults, shortcomings, ignorance, and disobedience and for making a way for my return. Thank you for staying close to me even when I strayed far from you. Thank you for keeping me, even when I didn't know I needed to be kept. Thank you for loving me when I didn't deserve your love. Thank you, Lord, for keeping me safe until the day of redemption through the power of the Holy Spirit who rules and reigns in my life.

WORD FOR THE DAY:

1 Peter 2:9 (KJV)
>But ye are a chosen generation, a royal priesthood, an holy nation, a peculiar people; that ye should shew forth the praises of him who hath called you out of darkness into his marvellous light:

JUNE 26

WORD FOR TODAY:

Proverbs 17:17 (KJV)
>A friend loveth at all times, and a brother is born for adversity.

JUNE 27

Stop trying to build your house on things outside of the word. Get with your family and get your house in order. Run it as the word of God teaches us. Dedicate and make your house a house of prayer. When people comes to visit, they will perceive something so different about your house. People will just know there is something different about your house and will respect the standard that is set. There is no way I would keep my natural house better than I keep my spiritual house. We must live life free from sin and live as if today is your last. If God has taken up invited residence in your soul, keep it in order. He can't dwell in an unclean vessel. Continue to ask God to teach you how to possess your vessel in holiness.

WORD FOR TODAY:

Psalm 127:1 (KJV)
> Except the Lord build the house, they labour in vain that build it: except the Lord keep the city, the watchman waketh but in vain.

JUNE 28

Success is not an accident—it's planned, it's intentional, and it's God's will. His plan is for us to prosper and be in health even as our soul prospers. While obtaining success, God is with us, He never leaves us. We mess up when we forget to include Him in our plans. We should never do anything without seeking council and approval from our Father. We must always participate and cooperate with the scripture. You will never be defeated if you incorporate God's word into your day. It is a light unto a path and a lamp unto our feet. We will see clearly our pathway as we pray about everything and worry about nothing. Every day, declare: "I'm not defeated. I'm more than a conqueror through Christ. I will look beyond my current circumstances to where God is taking me." You can make it. It might be rough at times but know that God will give you a victory in the end. Praise your way through. Run toward success. Success is planned and purposed. Winning is an attitude; defeat or failure is not an option.

Word for the Day:

Joshua 1:5, 8 (KJV)
> There shall not any man be able to stand before thee all the days of thy life: as I was with Moses, so I will be with thee: I will not fail thee, nor forsake thee. [8] This book of the law shall not depart out of thy mouth; but thou shalt meditate therein day and night, that thou mayest observe to do according to all that is written therein: for then thou shalt make thy way prosperous, and then thou shalt have good success.

June 29

The secret to prosperity, physically, spiritually, and financially, is God's word. Make sure you speak words of love, words of life, and speak and pray the word of God. The word of God will chase away all evil thinking, depression, defeat, sickness, and lack. The things that you meditate on are what you will react to. Meditate on God's word and have faith to know He will work all things out for your good, as He has declared in His word. He cannot lie.

You are where you are today as a result of what you did on yesterday (year). The decisions or seeds you sow now will bring forth much fruit to come. Sow good fruit with your words as well as your actions, and you will reap a great harvest. The enemy never attack you for where you are now but for where you are going.

Word for the Day:

Proverbs 18:21 (KJV)
> Death and life are in the power of the tongue: and they that love it shall eat the fruit thereof.

June 30

Imagine loving someone so deeply and so passionately, only to be walked away from. It hurts. It's so important to keep in mind and heart just how much God loves us and how much we love Him. We cannot take for granted the fact that He will always be with us. He will always provide and take care of us. He wants to hear words of love. God wants to see just how much you love Him through your acts of kindness for others. We must show His love to the homeless and the fatherless, those who are widows indeed. Ask yourself these questions: "Am I taking my God for granted? Am I showing forth His love to others? Are people seeing God in me?"

Word for Today:

Revelation 2:4 (KJV)
> Nevertheless I have somewhat against thee, because thou hast left thy first love.

TAKE AWAYS (NOTES)

JULY

Galatians 4:31 KJV - [31] So then, brethren, we are not children of the bondwoman, but of the free.

JULY 1

God never condemns us. He will never make us feel unworthy; it's the sin that condemns us and makes us feel unworthy of His love and forgiveness. It is the enemy's job to make us feel so unworthy that we would stay in sin longer than we intended to stay and pay way more than we intended to pay. God is good and His mercy is everlasting and His truth, His word, endures throughout all generations. We are not condemned; we are loved and are distributed kindness from God at all times.

WORD FOR TODAY:

Romans 8:1 KJV
[1] There is therefore now no condemnation to them which are in Christ Jesus, who walk not after the flesh, but after the Spirit.

July 2

Early in the morning will I seek the Lord, I shall pray and stay in His presence. It is in Him that I will trust, not in my own ability or strength. I can do nothing absent from Him. He is my refuge and my strength. I will allow Him to guide and lead my pathway today, knowing if I adhere to His voice, there are no wrong steps. He will keep my feet from stumbling, He will guide my tongue as the learned, and He shall keep me in perfect peace as I keep my mind stayed on Him.

Word for Today:

Psalm 5:2–3 KJV

[2] Hearken unto the voice of my cry, my King, and my God: for unto thee will I pray. [3] My voice shalt thou hear in the morning, O Lord; in the morning will I direct my prayer unto thee, and will look up.

July 3

I'm more convinced than ever that the word of God is my roadmap to success. So many times we try to go at life alone, and we listen to others' advice to determine what it is we should do to obtain satisfaction and success. They can only give you their advice based on what their experiences have been, only to find it proved unsuccessful. Why do you ask them? You are not them, and their journey is not yours. We must rely on God's word for guidance. Ask Him to lead, guide, and direct you in *all* of your endeavors. He has equipped us with everything we need to have good success and make our way prosperous. Make sure you are spending quality time with Him and saturating your spirit with His word daily. Just as the body needs food to be strong and healthy, our spirit man needs nourishment from the word of God to be strong and healthy. We need to talk with Him every step of the way. He will not lead you wrong. His ear is always attentive to you. He will give you the desires of your heart if you delight in Him. He has written your book—you win!

Word for Today:

Joshua 1:8 KJV
> [8] This book of the law shall not depart out of thy mouth; but thou shalt meditate therein day and night, that thou mayest observe to do according to all that is written therein: for then thou shalt make thy way prosperous, and then thou shalt have good success.

July 4

I will bless the Lord at all times, and His praises shall continue to be in my mouth. Throughout the day, every day, I will praise His holy name. I will condition my body, mind, and soul to show forth His praises. As my heart fills with the joy if His salvation and the promise of eternal life, I will praise Him. I know things are temporary and will not always exist. Nothing is this life is worthy to be compared to the glory that shall be revealed unto us. God is truly awesome and so worthy of my praise.

Word for Today:

John 4:23-24 KJV

[23] But the hour cometh, and now is, when the true worshippers shall worship the Father in spirit and in truth: for the Father seeketh such to worship him. [24] God is a Spirit: and they that worship him must worship him in spirit and in truth.

July 5

It doesn't matter what comes my way, I have been persuaded by God's word that I am an overcomer. I will endure hardship as a good soldier. I know there is nothing good that God will withhold from me. I am His child. I am royalty and kingdom. God is able to do exceedingly abundantly above all that I ask, think, or feel. He is truly awesome!

Word for Today:

Romans 8:38-39 KJV

[38] For I am persuaded, that neither death, nor life, nor angels, nor principalities, nor powers, nor things present, nor things to come, [39] Nor height, nor depth, nor any other creature, shall be able to separate us from the love of God, which is in Christ Jesus our Lord.

July 6

Why do you worry? Our Father will never neglect you, neither will he forsake you. Whatever you need He has it, He has everything you need and then some. If you put your trust in Him, walk by faith and not be what you see, and began to thank Him, before you know it you'll have whatever you're in need of. When we, as believers start putting in practice our faith, and stop allowing situations or circumstances to control our thoughts and actions, then and only then will we be pleasing in the eyes of our Father God. He promised to take care of us. We have benefits as His children and yes, you are entitled to them. God knows what we have need of before we ask Him, but we must open our mouth and ask, believe in our hearts to receive it.

Word for Today:

Matthew 6:25-27

> [25]"Therefore I tell you, do not worry about your life, what you will eat or drink; or about your body, what you will wear. Is not life more than food, and the body more than clothes? [26] Look at the birds of the air; they do not sow or reap or store away in barns, and yet your heavenly Father feeds them. Are you not much more valuable than they? [27]Can any one of you by worrying add a single hour to your life[e] ?

July 7

We must not allow sinful thoughts to persist; we must cast them down, and release them unto the Lord, and He will take them. We can't hide anything from Him. He knows our thoughts before we do, so confess them and leave them with Him. Otherwise, we will allow those impure thoughts into our hearts. Once they are conceived there, they will then be achieved through our actions. That's when they become sin. Nothing is worth the penalty you will have to pay. So, confess those thoughts and or desires, no matter how bad you may think they are. He already knows about them. God will take them, and as often as you have them, give them to God and get away from those circumstances that negatively affect your thinking.

Word for Today:

1 John 1:9 KJV

[9] If we confess our sins, he is faithful and just to forgive us our sins, and to cleanse us from all unrighteousness.

July 8

Growing in your faith towards Jesus is a must to live in this world. Theres no way to thrive and live a successful life without Him, especially when we have committed our lives to Him. Here is the faith challenge, trust God to do something so enormous that it would be an act of God for it to come to fruition. Remembering that God has given us access to the Kingdom,

He has given us the authority and power here in the earth to speak things into existence. So much so that whatever we say yes to in the earth, He says yes in Heaven and whatever we said no to in the earth, He says no in Heaven. Go ahead today, stretch your faith and allow God to do the supernatural. Open your business, buy that home, go get that degree, get into ministry training, etc. When God says yes, the answer is yes. God said yes you can, my child.

WORD FOR TODAY:

Matthew16:19 KJV
> [19] "I will give you the keys to the kingdom of heaven; whatever you bind on earth will be bound in heaven, and whatever you loose on earth will be loosed in heaven".

JULY 9

As the day progresses and situations compile, our natural tendencies would be to get caught up into the situation and forget to include God in the process of trying to find a solution. We must take time to seek His face and grace throughout the day. Take some quiet time to praise and reflect on His goodness and His omnipotence and ability to do anything but fail. When we get into His presence, answers will begin to surface with solutions that will always bring about positive results. Take advantage of God's supernatural ability to do the impossible. He is willing and able to do exceeding abundantly above all we can imagine.

SCENT OF HEAVEN

WORD FOR TODAY:

Deuteronomy 30:20 KJV

[20] That thou mayest love the Lord thy God, and that thou mayest obey his voice, and that thou mayest cleave unto him: for he is thy life, and the length of thy days: that thou mayest dwell in the land which the Lord sware unto thy fathers, to Abraham, to Isaac, and to Jacob, to give them.

Romans 12:2 KJV

[2] And be not conformed to this world: but be ye transformed by the renewing of your mind, that ye may prove what is that good, and acceptable, and perfect, will of God.

JULY 10

Everything is beautiful in the sight of God almighty. He created all things, and without Him was nothing made. There are no big I's nor little you's. Saints and sinners alike are precious to Him, and He loves us all. As Christians, we must always remember that God is love and His desire is for us to reach souls, to be His example of love in the earth. Let's embrace every creature of God with love and respect. If we should encounter those who may not fare as well as we do, we are to receive them with open arms and see how we can assist them. We all need God. He uses us to for His will, for His pleasure. Jesus died so that we all might receive salvation. We are saved by Jesus Christ, and to whomever will believe and receive His redeeming blood.

WORD FOR TODAY:

Acts 10:28
> God has shown me that I should not call any man common or unclean.

JULY 11

Just as Elijah asked God to open the young man's eyes so that he could see the horses and chariots of fire that were sent by God to fight the battle, we must also ask God to open up our spiritual vision so that we can see He presence in every challenge we face and to see that He is with us in every single victory we win. We are never alone; God will always be there to give us victory! He celebrates with us when we are praising Him and rejoicing. There is no force stronger than our God. If by chance we even have to fight in the battle, we are equipped with the armor of God and will not be defeated. It is to build our spiritual stamina and to see God's power at work in and through us. It's always for our good, never to harm us. There is no foe that could ever defeat us when we trust God.

WORD FOR TODAY:

2 Kings 6:16
> And Elisha prayed, and said, "LORD, I pray, open his eyes that he may see." Then the LORD opened the

eyes of the young man, and he saw. And behold, the mountain was full of horses and chariots of fire all around Elisha.

July 12

Do you even know what your benefit package includes? Everything! We must enjoy our endless benefits of being saved, washed in the pure blood of Jesus Christ our redeeming Savior. There's no other benefits comparable to it. We can make a request, and it will be granted unto us. We have power in His name, demons has to flee, sickness has to leave, and the darkness has to go. We must trust in Him no matter what our circumstances may be. God is the ultimate source of all our blessings; as such we must acknowledge Him and praise Him for all things.

Word for Today:

John 16:24 KJV
   [24] Hitherto have ye asked nothing in my name: ask, and ye shall receive, that your joy may be full.

July 13

Give the Lord each hour of every day to the Lord. Start each day in prayer in connecting with the Savior of our body and soul. He who knows the ending from the beginning. Seek His face for all things from the smallest to the greatest. He shall never fall short of His promises to us. His thoughts toward us are good, never bad. They are thoughts of peace and a successful end with life everlasting with Him. But while we are in this life, we must take advantage and enjoy our relationship with the Father. There's nothing good He will ever keep from us. He knows all of our needs and promises to supply them. Trust Him with all of you.

WORD FOR TODAY:

Psalm 37:5 KJV
[5] Commit thy way unto the Lord; trust also in him; and he shall bring it to pass.

JULY 14

When we put our trust in God, it leaves no room for doubt. We no longer trust in our own ability or intellect. It is He who dwells inside of us and gives us the ability to do, to have, and to be. We cannot take credit for all that God does through us. For in us (the flesh) dwells no good thing. It is only through Holy Spirit that we can do what is right and pleasing unto God. When it's beyond our fleshly comprehension, we must blindly trust God, knowing He is in control of the most challenging times of our lives, and He is working it in our favor. In those times when we can't sense His presence, we still must put our trust in Him, the one and only true God, our Father. It all comes together in the end.

Word for Today:

Proverbs 3:5-6 KJV

> [5] Trust in the Lord with all thine heart; and lean not unto thine own understanding. [6] In all thy ways acknowledge him, and he shall direct thy paths.

July 15

Oftentimes, we get caught up in what will or will not happen tomorrow, when we don't even know if there will be tomorrow. We put our faith in uncertain things instead of putting our faith and trust in the one who controls tomorrow, who knows exactly what we have need of and has promised to supply them according to His riches. It's not of our own accord that we attain success or even riches; it's only through God's power we are who we are, we have what we have, and we do the things that we do. We can with certainty depend on Him for everything. Even in the times of trouble, we can rejoice, knowing He has us and will not let us go.

Word for Today:

Matthew 6:34 KJV

> [34] Take therefore no thought for the morrow: for the morrow shall take thought for the things of itself. Sufficient unto the day is the evil thereof.

July 16

In times of trouble, when I feel despair or just helpless, God is there, and it is He who reaches down when I reach up, pulling me to a safe place and space in Him. We must trust Him, even when I can't trace Him. He is the unseen force who guides us through to safety. Whatever or whoever aided us into getting in that horrible place, we must learn what or who it was so that we may be on guard, lest we find ourselves back in that place, once again awaiting God's deliverance.

Word for Today:

Psalm 40:2-3 KJV
> [2] He brought me up also out of an horrible pit, out of the miry clay, and set my feet upon a rock, and established my goings. [3] And he hath put a new song in my mouth, even praise unto our God: many shall see it, and fear, and shall trust in the Lord.

July 17

The only way to know someone passionately, inside and out, is to spend time with them. Know who the love of your life is and invest time and resources getting to know them. The more you spend alone time with God, the more you will know Him, the better you will understand Him, and the more aware you will be of His presence in your life. His desire is to have intimate time with you so that you may know Him in His fullness. Realize that the time you spend with Him is far more precious and important than anything else you will do. Far too many times we spin our wheels, wasting time with everything and everybody instead of utilizing the time you have and making full use of it, strengthening your relationship with God for all eternity. Relationships and time here are temporary, but the time spent with God is everlasting, and that's what matters.

Word for Today:

Song of Songs 2:13 KJV
[13] The fig tree putteth forth her green figs, and the vines with the tender grape give a good smell. Arise, my love, my fair one, and come away.

July 18

We should feel God's presence all the time as we live close to Him. He is never far from us. It is in and through Him that we live, so just as we inhale air, we should inhale His fragrance. Know that it is Him who gives us life all through the day, giving praise for the life we have. When things aren't going as we have planned them, stop and seek God's direction. Implore His supernatural ability to show you what path to take. Make sure you pray about everything. It's in Him we have the activity of our limbs; we should never take that for granted. He is our ultimate and only source; He only uses others to help us but it is all in and through Him.

Word for Today:

Acts 17:27-28 KJV
> [27] That they should seek the Lord, if haply they might feel after him, and find him, though he be not far from every one of us: [28] For in him we live, and move, and have our being; as certain also of your own poets have said, For we are also his offspring.

July 19

Our weapons are not carnal; we don't use knives, guns, or even an evil tongue to fight our battles. Our weapon is the word of God and the word only. We must take the little faith that we have and use it to the best of our ability. Whenever the enemy throw his fiery darts, we must speak faith, using our tongue as our weapon to extinguish those darts. The only real and powerful weapon that will yield great results is our faith. We have so much power in our faith; we must use it to our advantage. God will never leave us unprotected. He is our protection, and His word will stand forever. Let's live by the word of God. Speak faith and quench every negative thought and every satanic attack the enemy will bring. We are more than conquerors.

Word for Today:

Ephesians 6:16 KJV
> [16] Above all, taking the shield of faith, wherewith ye shall be able to quench all the fiery darts of the wicked.

July 20

There's a place where God dwells in my soul that only He can satisfy. This world is not my home. It long to be in its natural inhabitant and until then, my soul will wait upon the deliverer of my soul. I am in Him, and He is in me. Without Him, I am nothing, and I can do nothing. My day begins and ends with God. Until He returns, I will patiently wait upon Him to redeem my total body, soul, and spirit in union with Him.

Word for Today:

Psalm 42:1-2 KJV

[1] As the hart panteth after the water brooks, so panteth my soul after thee, O God. [2] My soul thirsteth for God, for the living God: when shall I come and appear before God?

July 21

It's amazing that our Savior endured everything that we will ever endure. He is a perfect example for us as believers. Jesus felt all the emotions that we feel and was confronted with the same sins that we face, yet He did not sin. He did not sin because He knew we needed a spotless sacrifice. He knew His purpose, and He held fast to His convictions no matter how hard the temptation. He didn't just do any and everything that came along. He didn't even make any excuses so that we could have an example to pursue. We must say just as Jesus said, "Be it unto us according to my Father's will." What does it matter? Everything revolves around Him. He is our life, He is our source; He is our eternity. It's all about Him, working His will through us.

WORD FOR TODAY:

Luke 22:42 KJV
[42] Saying, Father, if thou be willing, remove this cup from me: nevertheless not my will, but thine, be done.

JULY 22

Everything we do, we must do for God's glory and not our own. We make the mistake of getting caught up into what people think about us or how people view us, which is not good. Our desire should be to please the Lord. God is our source, and every good deed we do or seed we sow is to God's glory. Someone will see or experience our Godly attributes and desire to make Jesus head of their lives. We will receive a great reward in Heaven, so don't expect anything from man. That way you won't desire to please them, neither will you be disappointed in their lack of appreciation and/or praise. Even the word tells us that a prophet isn't respected in his own country.

WORD FOR TODAY:

Matthew 6:1 KJV
[1] Take heed that ye do not your alms before men, to be seen of them: otherwise ye have no reward of your Father which is in heaven.

July 23

So many times we get so caught up in life's "busyness" that we failed to hear the voice of our Father speaking to us. We must spend time not just talking with God but allowing Him to speak to us, to encourage us, to instruct us, and sometimes even warn us. We get so accustomed to doing all the talking that we forget that He wants to talk as well. We have relationship with the Father, and as a result of our relationship, we must relate to one another. Take time to listen to Him, He has a word for you. It's call and response: when we call, He responds. We just have to take the time to listen as He admonishes, instructs, and give us insight for the road ahead of us.

Word for Today:

Psalm 81:8
> "Hear, O My people, and I will admonish you! O Israel, if you will listen to Me!

July 24

The password into God's presence is praise. If we want to experience a supernatural encounter with God, we must be thankful. In order to be a subject in His Kingdom, we must give Him praise. Our praise will take us through any door; it will take us over every high mountain. Our praise is the password to reach Heaven. So when we are tempted to complain, think of all of God's goodness toward you. And His mercy is brand new every day.

WORD FOR TODAY:

Psalm 100:4 KJV
[4] Enter into his gates with thanksgiving, and into his courts with praise: be thankful unto him, and bless his name.

JULY 25

As a Christian, there's nothing we go through that God doesn't have a hand in. We can do all things through Christ who gives us the victory. Just flip to the back of the book and see that we win. It will all work out for our good, and God will get the glory. Even when it seems it's not looking good and there's a turn in the wrong direction, just look unto the hills from which our help comes from, knowing that all of our help comes from the Lord. He is sending you the answer; things are turning around just for you. He will never let us down. He has called us for His purpose.

WORD FOR TODAY:

Romans 8:28 KJV
[28] And we know that all things work together for good to them that love God, to them who are the called according to his purpose.

July 26

I love the way freedom feels inside of me, I love the way it looks on me, and I love the way it moves me. Because we are free, we can be free to love others, no matter what they have done to us or to our loved ones. You see, we understand that when our enemies go low, we go high. It's not the physical act of the person that we fight with but that spiritual being that wants nothing more than to steal our freedom away. Unforgiveness is way too heavy to carry around. We understand that the enemy most times is the enemy within us, keeping us from having peace of mind and spirit. We must pray for our enemies that God will touch their hearts and fill them with His glorious presence. Let's help others to be free as we are free and free indeed.

Word for Today:

John 8:36 KJV
[36] If the Son therefore shall make you free, ye shall be free indeed.

July 27

If it's not you, O God, I don't want it, and I know I don't need it. More of you is what I need; as I need the air to breathe, I need you, God. You are the very air that I breathe, and without you, I cease to exist. For me to live is you and to die is to gain you for all eternity. Nothing in this life is worth my losing you; nothing is worth missing you. Your kingdom is my desire, and to please you each and every day is my desire. I only want to be pleasing in your sight. I will not fear man, only you, God. You are the key to my destiny, and I say yes all through the day. You can use me until you use me up, and then to spend eternity with you is my greatest desire. I thirst for you, for you are my water, the living well of water on the inside of me.

WORD FOR TODAY:

Psalm 42:2 KJV
>[2] My soul thirsteth for God, for the living God: when shall I come and appear before God?

JULY 28

Love is the principle thing, the core, the foundation of every action. No matter what you do in life, love should be the only motivating force behind it. If love is not the force behind your actions, it is for nothing. Guilt, regret, notoriety, unforgiveness, and so on will carry no weight in glory, only love. So in whatever seeds you sow, make sure they are sown in love, and they will grow up it in love. Remember, God is love.

WORD FOR TODAY:

1 John 4:18 KJV
>[18] There is no fear in love; but perfect love casteth out fear: because fear hath torment. He that feareth is not made perfect in love.

July 29

We must love the Lord with everything; we must love everybody as God is love. We can't love in word only, but we must love in deed. When we love God, we keep His commandments, we obey His word, and we honor Him in doing so. Even when we don't understand the things we suffer through or endure, we must love Him with everything, knowing He knows what's best and we don't. God loved us first, and He showed us by giving us life through His only Son, Jesus. He created a way for us to live when there was no way. We failed and were doomed to a Christless eternity in Hell, but God loved us so much, He couldn't stand to be separated from His children. Therefore, He sent Jesus as the ultimate sacrifice for sin. Because He loves and is love, He expects the same from His offsprings.

Word for Today:

Matthew 22:37 KJV
[37] Jesus said unto him, Thou shalt love the Lord thy God with all thy heart, and with all thy soul, and with all thy mind.

July 30

The Lord's desire is for us to see His beauty in everything. There's nothing ugly about God; beauty is defined by Him, and it is Him. Therefore, everything and everyone connected to Him is beautiful. He is the creator of beauty; even His arch enemy was a beautiful creation made by Him. We must see God's beauty in all that we do and give Him praise and honor.

WORD FOR TODAY:

Psalm 29:2 KJV
> [2] Give unto the Lord the glory due unto his name; worship the Lord in the beauty of holiness.

JULY 31

We are never alone; even when we are physically by ourselves, God is with us. He promised never to leave or forsake us. We must know He is always there, even inside us, to keep us until the end of time. He is the hope that resides in our internal being, that keeps us going and looking upward. It is in Him that we live, move, and have our being. Keep Him each and all day at the forefront of your life, talk to Him, and stay in His presence. There's no safer place to be.

WORD FOR TODAY:

Colossians 1:27 KJV
> [27] To whom God would make known what is the riches of the glory of this mystery among the Gentiles; which is Christ in you, the hope of glory:

TAKE AWAYS (NOTES)

AUGUST

Psalm 1:6 KJV - [6] For the Lord knoweth the way of the righteous: but the way of the ungodly shall perish.

AUGUST 1

Things will happen in life to deter us from focusing and serving God. It's a ploy of the enemy to turn us away from our God, but we must see through it. Know that God cares and we can't give up nor give out; it's not worth it. Nothing and nobody is worth your being separated from our God.

WORD FOR TODAY:

Romans 8:38-39 KJV

[38] For I am persuaded, that neither death, nor life, nor angels, nor principalities, nor powers, nor things present, nor things to come, [39] Nor height, nor depth, nor any other creature, shall be able to separate us from the love of God, which is in Christ Jesus our Lord.

AUGUST 2

The Lord wants us happy, His desire is for us to be glad and excited to be with Him to be a part of His Kingdom. He never forces us to do anything we don't want to do. Our heart should be lean on Him and only Him. He has so much more to offer, so much more in store for us. Our future is greater; it's brighter simply because He is in it. Each day is new and rewarding as we stay close to Him, talking to Him and giving Him reverence and enjoying His presence in our lives. Blessed are we to be in Him; He feels a love for us so deep that He was willing to die so that we could live. Ultimately, He knew we'd be together with Him.

WORD FOR TODAY:

Psalm 21:6 KJV
[6] For thou hast made him most blessed for ever: thou hast made him exceeding glad with thy countenance.

AUGUST 3

I'm reminded of the childhood song that says to "be careful little tongue what you speak, there's a God up above looking down with tender love, so be careful little tongue what you speak." Though the smallest member of the body, the tongue is the biggest evil there is. It can bless as well as curse; it can give life as well as death. It can change the course of nature, and it can change your future. We must consider everything that comes out of our mouths *before* it comes out of our mouth.

Don't lose control, but allow the holy fruit of self-control to control your tongue. God desires our voices as well as our bodies to be consecrated unto Him. We must speak what God tells us to speak. When He tells us to speak it, it's a matter of life and death. Life and death are in the power of your tongue, so speak life.

WORD FOR TODAY:

Ephesians 4:29 KJV
> [29] Let no corrupt communication proceed out of your mouth, but that which is good to the use of edifying, that it may minister grace unto the hearers.

AUGUST 4

Isn't it something that Jesus didn't stop Satan from pursuing Peter, nor did He command him to leave Peter alone? He prayed for Peter; why? Sometimes we just have to face our demons and destroy them in order that we can see and know that we are much more powerful than the enemy is. It's for us to learn that we can do all things through the power of God who dwells within us. The best teacher is experience; through our experience, we are effective witnesses of the victory that awaits us after going through. Have you ever asked for help and the response was, "I'm praying for you"? Just imagine Jesus saying to you, "The enemy desires to have you, but I'm praying for you because once you get victory over him, you need to help others who are experiencing the same challenge." Stop waiting on the Lord and step out in faith. God is moved

SCENT OF HEAVEN

by your faith in Him. He loves it when you operate with holy boldness, knowing that you're not fighting this battle just for yourself but for you to help others.

WORD FOR TODAY:

Luke 22:32 KJV
 [32] But I have prayed for thee, that thy faith fail not: and when thou art converted, strengthen thy brethren.

AUGUST 5

Once we accept Christ as our Savior, we receive His Holy Spirit. We are then united as one with Him. We are the inheritors of everything God has and everything Jesus has. All things belong to us as being double heirs on the throne. Because He sits and reigns, we should also rule and reign. Therefore, whatever we declare and decree is established. We can walk in the blessed assurance that the word of God will never fail. He will keep His word and shall keep what we commit unto Him. We belong to God, so do not fret anything, anyone, or any circumstance. God is a rewarder of us who diligently seek Him. Seek His approval or disapproval for all that you do, for He is our Father, and we should honor His word. He knows what is best for us.

WORD FOR TODAY:

Romans 8:16-18 KJV
 [16] The Spirit itself beareth witness with our spirit, that we are the children of God: [17] And if children, then

heirs; heirs of God, and joint-heirs with Christ; if so be that we suffer with him, that we may be also glorified together. [18] For I reckon that the sufferings of this present time are not worthy to be compared with the glory which shall be revealed in us.

AUGUST 6

What a friend we have in Jesus, I'm persuaded that there's no other friend who will compare to Him. What friend do you know who will actually do what Jesus did? I don't even know if my loved one would do what He did for us. He did it because He was so in love with us, so He gave His life for us. He was beaten, torn, and killed just for us. What a friend we have in Jesus. He loves us at all times; yes, even when we didn't love Him, He still loved us—undeserving us. He saw beyond our many faults and saw our need for Him. We must do the same for our friends, showing them Christ who lives on the inside of us so that they too can come to know the friend that you have in Him.

WORD FOR TODAY:

June 15:15
> No longer do I call you servants, for a servant does not know what his master is doing; but I have called you friends, for all things that I heard from My Father I have made known to you.

AUGUST 7

Many are called to Christ, but only a few are chosen. You were chosen to bear the name of Jesus to the unbeliever. It is incumbent upon us to share the good news of Jesus Christ to the world that doesn't know Him or believe in His existence. The best way for us to share Him with others is through a life sold out for Him. When the unbeliever sees us, they should see Jesus. As God sent Jesus into the world to be the light, we too are in the world as a light. Shine your light because someone somewhere is in search of the light. Every day, ask God to send someone your way so that you may be a witness for Him.

WORD FOR TODAY:

20:21
   As the Father has sent Me, I also send you.

AUGUST 8

Oftentimes we feel so unworthy, not deserving of God's kingdom inheritance. We are the righteousness of God because Jesus became sin for us to prove that sin no longer has power or dominion over us. Every day we must renew our minds and know that we have been accepted in the Beloved. Stop giving place to wrongdoing; the enemy no longer controls our thoughts, but Holy Spirit does. We are one body in Christ; we are royalty. As such, we must put off all things that are not of Christ, being renewed daily. Jesus loves us as we are because

He sees the finished product. We are His bride and are beautiful in His eyes.

WORD FOR TODAY:

Isaiah 61:10 KJV
> [10] I will greatly rejoice in the Lord, my soul shall be joyful in my God; for he hath clothed me with the garments of salvation, he hath covered me with the robe of righteousness, as a bridegroom decketh himself with ornaments, and as a bride adorneth herself with her jewels.

AUGUST 9

In order to get to any destination, you must have a road map, a compass, or know how to get there. Otherwise, you wander around, getting nowhere. You're lost with no sense of direction or belonging. God gave us His word to be our spiritual road map to eternal life. We need it to know where we are going daily. There's no way to walk this Christian journey without the direction of God's word. It's His home, and He knows the way to get there. That's why we should look only to Him for direction to His Eternal Home. Each day, we must make full use of His roadmap; we never know when it will be our last day. God knows, so He tells us to appreciate and make full use of our time because each day is evil, full of distractions and warfare from the enemy to throw us off our destination. Get in the word and stay in the word, and we will arrive at our eternal heavenly destination, with a host of angels to usher us to our mansion.

Word for Today:

Ephesians 5:15-16 KJV
> [15] See then that ye walk circumspectly, not as fools, but as wise, [16] Redeeming the time, because the days are evil.

August 10

My mother would always use the phrase, "I give because I have but more than that, I have because I give." I didn't understand that phrase as a child, but as an adult, I realize it's not a phrase — it's a standard of living and giving. How many times have we gotten all that we can and kept it all for ourselves? We did that in selfish unbelief. The law principle in reaping and gathering has always been and will always be. We must be willing to give even when it hurts. That is when faith in God steps in, and undoubtedly you know with everything within you that God will reward you for the seeds that you have sown. When you sow, you reap more bountifully than you've sown. So never neglect to give; when we give, it is restored back in overflow.

Word for Today:

Acts 11:29
> Then the disciples, each according to his ability, determined to send relief to the brethren dwelling in Judea.

AUGUST 11

There's is nothing we can do to pay Jesus back for the gift of salvation. We were not worthy and will never be able to repay Him. His desire for us is to be humble and obedient unto Him, not for His good but for our own good. We shall all be rewarded for the things that we have done. As we stand before the judgment seat of Christ, we shall be rewarded, not condemned. We aren't saved because we have done a work for Him, we do a work for Him because we are saved and He has commanded us to spread His word. Just as He loves us, and He loves the sinner. He hates the acts of sin but loves the sinner. Let us obey our Father in word and in our deeds so that others will come to know His redeeming power of salvation. His desire is for no flesh to be lost.

WORD FOR TODAY:

Ephesians 2:8
> By grace you have been saved through faith, and that not of yourselves; it is the gift of God, not of works, lest anyone should boast.

AUGUST 12

It's imperative that we allow time for Holy Spirit to commune with God. It is a need, not just a want. We will go through things. We will have hardships and battles after battles. The spirit already knows what is to come as well as what we need for the present time. Take some quality time to spend with

God; give up, give in, let go, and let the Holy Spirit speak on your behalf. It's as simple as opening your mouth in prayer in total surrender, in worship, and He will began to speak. God knows and understand our weakness, and He wants to heal us where we hurt — but we must let Him. We can't heal ourselves, especially when the hurt is so deep and fresh. He feels all our infirmities, and He desires to make us like new. Let Him.

WORD FOR TODAY:

Romans 8:26 KJV

[26] Likewise the Spirit also helpeth our infirmities: for we know not what we should pray for as we ought: but the Spirit itself maketh intercession for us with groanings which cannot be uttered.

AUGUST 13

Life is for the living. Jesus died, yes, that we might have eternal life with Him but also that we may live this life in abundance. Many times we go through life, just eagerly awaiting the destination but never stopping or taking a moment to enjoy the journey. Life is a journey full of surprises, not all good. Even in those unexpected moments, take a minute to reflect, to exhale, and to seize the day. Take note of the scenery. Nothing just happens. We must receive the gift of life that our God has given us and never take it for granted. We must enjoy the people we meet, the children we rear, the job we don't like, and the spouses we are sharing our deepest moments with. Challenges will come, but God has empowered us with all we need to be successful, to be more than conquers. Chose to be happy and accept the gift of life with joy and peace. Every day should to be lived as though it is your last.

Word for Today:

John 10:10-11 KJV
> [10] The thief cometh not, but for to steal, and to kill, and to destroy: I am come that they might have life, and that they might have it more abundantly. [11] I am the good shepherd: the good shepherd giveth his life for the sheep.

AUGUST 14

He will do far greater things than our minds could imagine or than we can fix our mouths to utter; that's the God whom we serve. God never takes anything away from us without replacing it with something far greater than we had before. The power and authority that He has given us is not limited. God does not fit into a box, and neither do we. The extent of the power and authority He has given to us cannot be measured. Heaven is the limit, and that's only because that's where our God dwells. We must know His word — the word makes us powerful. God is the word, and because He is, we are. Let's use the power and the authority that has been given to us by the Creator of all things.

Word for Today:

Ephesians 3:20
> To Him who is able to do exceedingly abundantly above all that we ask or think, according to the power that works in us.

August 15

The tongue can get unruly sometimes as we know. That's why it's so important that we allow our tongue to be tamed by the Holy Spirit. Make sure we are not just hearers but we are actually listening attentively when something is being said. We should ask God to give us what we should utter, so that He might be pleased. Many times we talk without really listening to what is being said; we must hear with our spiritual ears. Seeking God's council on how to respond is including Him into the conversation, and your response will be His response. Hear God's voice as He speaks to you and then respond; it will prove to be the right reply.

Word for Today:

James 1:19 KJV
> [19] Wherefore, my beloved brethren, let every man be swift to hear, slow to speak, slow to wrath.

AUGUST 16

If we abide in God's word and His word abides in us, we would live a prosperous and healthy life physically and spiritually. The problem becomes crucial when we aren't spending ample time with Him and in Him. He is where life is; He is the very air that we inhale but the last thing we want to commit to. When we think of good thoughts, that's God; when we can do ministry, that's God; when we can give a word or act of kindness, that's God. It helps us to stay strong and healthy mentally, physically, and spiritually. Too many times we are distracted by the darts that are thrown our way, get out of spiritual

character, and resort to fleshly actions we soon regret. However, all that did was throw us off of what God has appointed for us to do. We must stay focused on what is right and pleasing unto God, and be obedient to His word. He has given us the power to stay strong and be victorious.

WORD FOR TODAY:

Philippians 4:8 KJV
> [8] Finally, brethren, whatsoever things are true, whatsoever things are honest, whatsoever things are just, whatsoever things are pure, whatsoever things are lovely, whatsoever things are of good report; if there be any virtue, and if there be any praise, think on these things.

AUGUST 17

What an awesome God and Savior we have. He is the one who knows me by my name, and He has no respect of persons. Just as He loved Abraham, Isaac, and Jacob and was with them, so as He is with me. We are so blessed to having such a loving and caring God who loves us all and sees us a one body. We never have to worry about Him getting too busy for us, He takes personal interest and have the same love for each of us. We must see Him for the omnipotent, omnipresent God with agape love for us individually as well as collectively.

WORD FOR TODAY:

Isaiah 43:1 KJV
> [1] But now thus saith the Lord that created thee, O Jacob, and he that formed thee, O Israel, Fear not: for I have redeemed thee, I have called thee by thy name; thou art mine.

AUGUST 18

Do you make it a habit of opening the doors for your little ones, or even giving them the things that they ask you for? I believe the answer to that is yes. We are responsible for them. We are to ensure that they have all they need to sustain life, and we will go beyond that and give them some of the things they ask us for. God is far more gracious than we are. Ask—Seek—Knock are the only instructions God gives us. Our Father is obligated to give us when we ask, to receive when we seek

Him, and when we knock, the door will open unto us. With man it may be impossible, but with God all things are possible. He's waiting for you to ask. He's looking for you to seek Him, and He's at the door waiting for you to knock. That's the condition: you do your part, and He will do His.

WORD FOR TODAY:

Matthew 7:7-8 KJV
> [7] Ask, and it shall be given you; seek, and ye shall find; knock, and it shall be opened unto you: [8] For every one that asketh receiveth; and he that seeketh findeth; and to him that knocketh it shall be opened.

AUGUST 19

My soul rejoices, and my spirit is made glad when I'm in His presence. God has a way of making me feel just right. Even when my way seems dim, He brightens my path. If you just don't forget to go to God, to seek His face, to pray, and to praise and worship Him, you will find peace and joy in the midst of your storm. God will envelope you in His arms and allow you to feel His presence and wholeness.

WORD FOR TODAY:

Psalm 21:6 KJV
> [6] For thou hast made him most blessed for ever: thou hast made him exceeding glad with thy countenance.

AUGUST 20

Who says we aren't in control when the Holy Spirit gives us self-control; it's on the inside of us. So when we get angry and say or do things that are not pleasing to God, we grieve Holy Spirit. Even then, once we calm down and listen, His still, quiet voice begins to minister to us and convicts the actions that came along with our anger. Anger, but sin not, is what God tells us. You don't know what tomorrow will bring. So, don't allow anger to take root during the night. When anger is sown, unforgiveness springs forth, and if not cast down, we find ourselves displaying more displeasing actions. Listen to the Holy Spirit, repent of the action, and don't do it again. No one or nothing is worth your soul. I can't began to tell you how great the results will be. Learn from it.

WORD FOR TODAY:

Ephesians 4:26 KJV
   [26] Be ye angry, and sin not: let not the sun go down upon your wrath:

AUGUST 21

The thief wants to take what isn't his. He wants everything God has, is, and will be. Satan desires it and will try to obtain it by any means necessary. However, God has freely given us Himself freely, and we can enter in only through Jesus. Let us humbly walk through the doors that are open unto us and receive the abundant life that has already been prepared for us. There's no faking it; we must be real when we come to God. He knows our hearts and our thoughts before we ever utter a word, He knows what we will say. Open your heart unto God, and close your ears and eyes to the enemy, who is good at giving us false hopes and even showing smoke screens of things that aren't real to draw us in. But he can only do that if we do not know our Father's voice. Know God intimately so that you can know His voice when He is speaking to you, leading, directing and sometimes pleading with you. The enemy wants to steal, kill, and destroy by first getting into your spirit and ultimately destroying your soul, stealing you from God. Again, know your Father's voice; only then will you be able to ascertain the enemy's voice when he is speaking to you.

No matter what we face, we are never alone. All we have to do is ask in faith, and God shall fulfill it. No matter how bad the situation looks, you must believe He will deliver you. There is nothing too hard for God, and I promise you, nothing takes Him by surprise. Though we may be thrown off by things, we must maintain our composure and think and act as Christ would. All things will work out for our good. He will never leave nor forsake us. His promises are sure. Heaven and earth will pass, but God's word will abide forever. Trust God to work out your situation, no matter how big or small. God has you covered; just don't forget to ask. Some things God just wants you to ask and believe that you might receive, and He will get the glory. Always maintain your integrity in Christ and be ready for the unknown. In this world we must have on the whole armor of God because you never know when you will be under attack. Remember the greater the attack, the greater the anointing. Your healing is but a prayer away, your breakthrough is but a prayer away, and your deliverance is but a prayer away. God is able and will supply *all*.

WORD FOR TODAY:

John 10:8-10

> All that ever came before me are thieves and robbers: but the sheep did not hear them. [9] am the door: by me if any man enter in, he shall be saved, and shall go in and out, and find pasture. [10] The thief cometh not, but for to steal, and to kill, and to destroy: I am come that they might have life, and that they might have it more abundantly.

AUGUST 22

We must be totally submitted unto God so that when the enemy comes, we have the power in the name of Jesus to resist sin and bind up the hand of the enemy. Jesus rendered him powerless, so don't give him the credit that Jesus died for. He died so that we could have power over the enemy. You have the Holy Spirit and weapons far beyond anything he can use. You will not be defeated; you will not surrender. You will use your weapon (word) to resist him, and he has to go.

WORD FOR TODAY:

James 4:7 KJV
> [7] Submit yourselves therefore to God. Resist the devil, and he will flee from you.

AUGUST 23

For we walk by faith, not by sight. And the peace of God that is far greater than we can understand will keep your heart and mind. In the course of a day, so much transpires that it's hard to stay focus on Him. However, God wants us to step away from the busyness and step to Him and seek His face, for in Him only will you find peace. It will keep your heart and mind from the stresses that a day will bring. Only through and with Him can you even deal with all the challenges that come. Know that God is present and will help you; just take a minute to think of Him and ask in faith, without doubting, and He will lead you beside the still waters.

WORD FOR TODAY:

John 16:33 KJV
> [33] These things I have spoken unto you, that in me ye might have peace. In the world ye shall have tribulation: but be of good cheer; I have overcome the world.

August 24

Who wouldn't serve a God so gracious and true? No matter what our sins are, He is just to forgive us and will cast them into the sea of forgetfulness. He heals us of not just some but all of our iniquities, those things that we don't even want to remember because it was such gross behavior. God isn't concerned about any of that old stuff we did when we didn't know Him. He is only looking at what we will do as a believer. Don't allow the enemy to bring up your past without reminding him of his soon coming destiny. You remind him that you have been redeemed by the shed blood of the lamb, Jesus the Christ. Remind him that our Father has given us a crown of love, kindness, and mercy. Let your enemy hear the good news of Jesus Christ coming from your lips and as you give Him the word of God, your strength will immediately renewed.

Word for Today:

Psalm 103:3 KJV
> [3] Who forgiveth all thine iniquities; who healeth all thy diseases; [4] Who redeemeth thy life from destruction; who crowneth thee with lovingkindness and tender mercies; [5] Who satisfieth thy mouth with good things; so that thy youth is renewed like the eagle's

August 25

There was a book written some years ago entitled *The Secret*. My first response was, it's not a secret what God can do, has done, and will do. The power of positive thinking is biblical truths that if read and obeyed, unlocks the door of life and peace. God reveals to us His holiness, His supernatural ability to do what no other can do. He has revealed to us the truth of His word by many signs and wonders. We are His workmanship. Do you remember from whence you've come? He has done great things and has proven what is not a secret to His children.

WORD FOR TODAY:

Deuteronomy 29:
> [29] The secret things belong unto the Lord our God: but those things which are revealed belong unto us and to our children forever, that we may do all the words of this law.

AUGUST 26

God always finishes what He starts. He saved you, He filled you with His Spirit, and He has empowered you with at least a gift or two. Don't allow the gifts to lie dormant; use them or lose them. God commanded for us to do His will, and He will never put more on us than we are capable of handling. Use your gifts and talents unto the service of the Lord; it won't be in vain. As you operate in your gifting, it shows God you are capable of handling your gifts, He then is free to give you more.

WORD FOR TODAY:

Philippians1:6
> He who has begun a good work in you will complete it until the day of Jesus Christ..

AUGUST 27

If we say God is our leader and our guide, then we must continually stay in His presence throughout each and every day. How do we do this, you ask. We must constant pray, read, and meditate on His word, lest we walk in darkness and stumble or worse—fall. His word is the way, it's truth, and it's light and life.

WORD FOR TODAY:

Psalm 119:105
> Thy word is a lamp unto me feet and a light unto my pathway.

AUGUST 28

God is our peace. He will keep us in perfect peace as we keep our mind on Him. Life throws us curves, daggers, blind swipes, and so forth. We don't have to fear or be anxious about the unknown because we know God. We are His children, and He will keep us safe from harm. We will survive and succeed as more than conquerors because we are vigilant in and through Christ. We have the total package: God, Jesus, and the Holy Spirit. What or who shall prevail against such power? Not only do we have goodness and mercy forever, we have the Trinity forever. Stay in His presence as much as possible, and nothing, I mean nothing, will take you unprepared. God is our source, our foundation!

WORD FOR TODAY:

Psalm 4:6-8 KJV
> [6] There be many that say, Who will shew us any good? Lord, lift thou up the light of thy countenance upon us. [7] Thou hast put gladness in my heart, more than in the time that their corn and their wine increased. [8] I will both lay me down in peace, and sleep: for thou, Lord, only makest me dwell in safety.

AUGUST 29

God didn't want Abraham's son Isaac, God wanted his obedience. Abraham trust God, and he believed His promise. God said to Abraham, now I know you put me first. Yes, God knew, but Abraham had to know he could pass the ultimate test. Can God say the same thing about you as He said to Moses, "Now I know you put me first"? Without faith, it's impossible to please God. We must take hold of our day and command it and not allow the day to take hold of us. God word is our sustainer.

Word for Today:

Luke 12:23-26 KJV

[23] The life is more than meat, and the body is more than raiment. [24] Consider the ravens: for they neither sow nor reap; which neither have storehouse nor barn; and God feedeth them: how much more are ye better than the fowls? [25] And which of you with taking thought can add to his stature one cubit? [26] If ye then be not able to do that thing which is least, why take ye thought for the rest?

August 30

Do you really believe in the Omnipotence of God, the Omnipresence of God, and the Omniscience of God? Before everything was, He is; that is incomprehensible, but true. Heaven and earth will pass, but God's word shall abide forever. What that tells us is that God can do anything, God is everywhere, and He knows all things; there's nothing hidden from Him. He wants us to believe that He can do anything but fail you. He has never and will never fail us, so bring your challenges, disappointments, diseases, and infirmities. Bring it all, and lay it at His feet. He will take it upon your release, and you'll never be the same again. Only believe.

WORD FOR TODAY:

Hebrews 11:6 KJV

> [6] But without faith it is impossible to please him: for he that cometh to God must believe that he is, and that he is a rewarder of them that diligently seek him

AUGUST 31

Why put off things for the next day when it's within your ability to go ahead and complete the task? Always finish what you start; never leave things undone. Do all that is within your heart to do. God is faithful to give you the strength to complete it, according to His will. "If it is God's will" is always appropriate to say. Why, you ask? The word has declared, it's not within your power to speak what you will do tomorrow or the next moment—tomorrow or the next moment may never come. Life is but a vapor of smoke, which appears but a moment and soon vanishes.

WORD FOR TODAY:

James 4:13-15 KJV

> [13] Go to now, ye that say, To day or to morrow we will go into such a city, and continue there a year, and buy and sell, and get gain: [14] Whereas ye know not what shall be on the morrow. For what is your life? It is even a vapour, that appeareth for a little time, and then vanisheth away. [15] For that ye ought to say, If the Lord will, we shall live, and do this, or that.

TAKE AWAYS (NOTES)

SEPTEMBER

Psalm 119:77 KJV - [77] Let thy tender mercies come unto me, that I may live: for thy law is my delight.

SEPTEMBER 1

When Paul tells us to work out our salvation with fear and trembling, he means that we are to give careful attention to our actions and behavior, making sure that we represent the One who saved us with honor and humility. We must live each day as it would please our God. When we are obedient to His will, we will then be working out our salvation. Communicating with Him is key, obeying His command is vital, and living righteously will become second nature. It will be who you are and not what you do.

WORD FOR TODAY:

Philippians 2:12
    Work out your own salvation with fear and trembling.

SEPTEMBER 2

I remember when growing up listening to this evangelist on the radio and at the end of each message he would declare,

"You don't have any problems; all you need is faith in God." That stuck with me as a child. God will always give us all that we need, when we need it. He's always on time no matter how we try to push Him to do it when we want Him to. He does it in His own time. He is time, and He's in control of our lives and all that we face on a minute-by-minute basis. He promised to never leave us, nor forsake us. He's our ultimate provider, working through man, but He also provides for us miraculously. When we face challenges beyond our control, like a good Father, He steps in and helps us as we obey His word.

Word for Today:

Psalm 1:3
> He shall be like a tree planted by the rivers of water, that brings forth its fruit in its season, whose leaf also shall not wither; and whatever he does shall prosper.

September 3

Have you ever wondered why there's never a dull moment? The enemy has created such a busyness in our lives that it removes our focus on what is really important and really matters. God should always be an integral part of our day. We should first and foremost begin our day with Him by thanking Him for our present. We should end the day with Him by thanking Him for allowing us to enjoy the present among all other things he's blessed us with. We should take time throughout the day to inquire of Him as to how to handle every situation and stay focused on His presence within us. Then everything will fall into place. Stop, exhale, and pray.

WORD FOR TODAY:

Luke 10:39-42 KJV
> [39] And she had a sister called Mary, which also sat at Jesus' feet, and heard his word. [40] But Martha was cumbered about much serving, and came to him, and said, Lord, dost thou not care that my sister hath left me to serve alone? bid her therefore that she help me. [41] And Jesus answered and said unto her, Martha, Martha, thou art careful and troubled about many things: [42] But one thing is needful: and Mary hath chosen that good part, which shall not be taken away from her.

SEPTEMBER 4

Just as David was secure in knowing that no matter what is going on, no matter what I'm going through, God is able to give me peace and safety. Don't allow the difficult times to shake your faith and cause you to fear. If God be for you, He is far greater than an army against you. We must rest in knowing God knows all, He sees all, and He is everywhere. He will protect you at all times, and in the end you'll see He worked it out for your good. Rest in His unwavering love and protection.

WORD FOR TODAY:

Psalms 4:8

[8] I will both lie down in peace, and sleep; for You alone, O LORD, make me dwell in safety.

September 5

Word for Today:

Isaiah 61:3 KJV
> [3] To appoint unto them that mourn in Zion, to give unto them beauty for ashes, the oil of joy for mourning, the garment of praise for the spirit of heaviness; that they might be called trees of righteousness, the planting of the Lord, that he might be glorified.

September 6

Do we really understand the fact that everything on the face of this earth, seen or unseen, belongs to our Father God of the universe? Why fret over trivial things? Take all of your needs to God in prayer. There is nothing He will withhold from His children. Satan is the prince and power of the air, but the air belongs to God. He is still in control and will forever have authority, and so do we.

Word for Today:

Psalm 24:1
> The earth is the LORD's, and all its fullness.

Ephesians 2:2
> Occasionally, you may hear a teaching that claims this world is the property of Satan, obtained in the Fall (Gen. 3). Don't believe it. This world always has been and always will be God's. He will never relinquish His sovereignty to anyone.

SEPTEMBER 7

God is eager to show Himself to you. He is waiting with expectancy for you to bring your all to Him. He desires to teach us all there is to know about Him and desires to show us the paths of righteousness and lead us by His light. We are the light of this world; when men see us, they should see Him. He will do great and marvelous works through us for His name's sake. If we wait and not get in front of Him, He will show us what we don't see, and He will tell us what we don't hear.

WORD FOR TODAY:

Psalm 25:4-5
> Show me Your ways, O LORD; teach me Your paths. Lead me in Your truth ... for You are the God of my salvation; on You I wait all the day.

SEPTEMBER 8

Weeping may endure for a night, but joy comes in the morning. We all get a moment to grieve, be disappointed, or even be angry, but we must get over it. God will always offer us the means to snap out of our emotional restraints, whatever they be. Just as we don't like to see our loved ones suffer or feel bad, how much more do you think God feels about us? Our momentary distress is only for a moment. God will

turn our bad times into a time of joy, and what we thought was meant to destroy us actually brings us new life. What we thought was a curse ends up a blessing. He will turn things around for us if we allow Him to. He wants to see us joyful, so He can dance with us.

Word for Today:

Psalm 30:11
> You have turned for me my mourning into dancing; You have put off my sackcloth and clothed me with gladness.

September 9

Word for Today:

Psalm 25:4–5 KJV
> [4] Shew me thy ways, O Lord; teach me thy paths. [5] Lead me in thy truth, and teach me: for thou art the God of my salvation; on thee do I wait all the day.

September 10

Our natural mind cannot began to ascertain all the things God has in store for us who love Him and have committed our lives to Him. God desires to use us in ways that we can't begin to know until we open up and ask Him to use us for His glory and honor. He will perform the impossible, take the natural you and do a supernatural work through you. Holy Spirit quickens us and teaches us what to do, what to say, and communes with God on our behalf with utterances that cannot be understood by us though He and God know. Allow God to open your eyes and ears so that you can work the works of Him who chose us.

Word for Today:

1 Corinthians 2:9, 10
> Eye has not seen, nor ear heard ... the things which God has prepared for those who love Him. But God has revealed them to us through His Spirit. For the Spirit searches all things, yes, the deep things of God.

September 11

Our God is so amazing, His love is always certain. He will always be there for us, even when we don't deserve Him, and His love supersedes our wrong. His love and grace will never end; we will spend eternity with Him, and His love will still be the same. Today we remember the tragedy of 9/11, and I still see God's love and amazing grace, while there were so many fatalities, there was still so much love and coming together as a nation of people. So many times we want to ask why. But as in all things, in time, God will clarify as we trust Him in all things.

WORD FOR TODAY:

Psalm 102:27 KJV
   [27] But thou art the same, and thy years shall have no end.

SEPTEMBER 12

The word of God is more powerful than any man-made weapons. When we try and solve things with weapons of this world, we make a bigger mess of things. We must realize the enemy is not that person, but the devil, who uses other people to get you into things that you will regret and act upon impulse. We must use the word to our advantage, all we have to do is take it to the Lord in prayer, knowing that nothing is too difficult for Him to solve. He is far bigger than any problems you may have, whether with people or situations. We must trust God. He already knew the situation would occur and has equipped you with all you need to win this battle spiritually. Your ultimate goal in life is to win souls for Christ.

WORD FOR TODAY:

2 Corinthians 10:4 KJV
   [4] (For the weapons of our warfare are not carnal, but mighty through God to the pulling down of strong holds.

SEPTEMBER 13

We must never take our Lord God, Creator, Potter, Shepherd, for granted. So many times we get in our own way and think we can reprove or question God; that is an extreme no-no. God is all and knows all, and He is the one who created you and knows all there ever will be to know about you.

WORD FOR TODAY:

Romans 9:20-21 KJV
> [20] Nay but, O man, who art thou that repliest against God? Shall the thing formed say to him that formed it, Why hast thou made me thus? [21] Hath not the potter power over the clay, of the same lump to make one vessel unto honour, and another unto dishonour?

SEPTEMBER 14

God loves us so much that we are constantly on His mind. He is always looking for ways to bless us. He want us to think about Him just as He thinks of us. He desire for us to know just how deep His love, grace, and mercy goes for us. It's far deeper than any ocean. We are His, and He is ours; the relationship that we have with Him is incomparable with everything else He has created or made. We are His heartbeat. He gives us His undivided attention at all times; even when He is silent, He is thinking of us.

WORD FOR TODAY:

Psalms 8:4
> [4] What is man that You are mindful of him, and the son of man that You visit him?

September 15

God loves us so much and desires for us to live life and live in peace, not war. We must rest in His unfailing love for us, knowing He is proud to call us His children and He favors us above others. His thoughts of us are pure and kind to do us good and never evil. Each day embrace it with His love and affection and walk proud, keeping your head to the sky, knowing God loves us and sings our praises as well.

Word for Today:

Zephaniah 3:17 KJV
> [17] The Lord thy God in the midst of thee is mighty; he will save, he will rejoice over thee with joy; he will rest in his love, he will joy over thee with singing.

September 16

You are the apple of God's eyes. You put a twinkle in them and the beat in His heart. How can we neglect such great love? Whenever you feel unwanted, not loved, taken advantage of, mistreated, neglected, or whatever negative emotions the enemy tries to overtake you with, think about the fact that God said you are the apple of His eye and He will forever hide you under His strong wings of love. His love for us is all-sufficient.

WORD FOR TODAY:

Psalm 17:8
>Keep me as the apple of Your eye; hide me under the shadow of Your wings.

SEPTEMBER 17

Freedom is our privilege and our God-given right. There shouldn't be anything or anyone holding us down or caging us into a confined box. Our God is free, and He has made us free and free indeed. Why do we limit ourselves by thinking we can't do something when our God said we can do all things through Jesus Christ? The Holy Spirit gives us self-control so that we know our worldly limits. We are under the unction of His Spirit who lives on the inside of us, leading and guiding us into all truth and righteousness. Use your freedom liberally in Christ, but don't use your liberty as a basis to sin. We don't have to be confined or defined by anyone except our Creator, our Savior. His word says I am free, never to be bound again.

WORD FOR TODAY:

Psalm 32:9
>Do not be like the horse or like the mule, which have no understanding, which must be harnessed with bit and bridle, else they will not come near you

September 18

In all things we must seek God's face for His guidance and direction; we should do nothing in isolation of Him. When we include God in our decision making, it makes for a better outcome every time. When we do this, we are pleasing in His sight, and He will never give us wrong directives. Even when things don't go as we want them to, we know that all things work for our good, and that particular request was not in His plans. For we are the righteousness of God; everything we do, all that we say, or hope to be, should always be to please Him.

Word for Today:

Matthew 6:33 KJV
> [33] But seek ye first the kingdom of God, and his righteousness; and all these things shall be added unto you.

September 19

We must constantly commune with God; yes, even in our busyness, we must talk to Him. Ask for direction and guidance. When we stay in constant communication with Him, He is apt to fulfill our request, and we are less likely to make mistakes and wrong choices. God is here, right here with us, so seek Him honestly and earnestly and get fulfilled results. You can't go wrong by staying right in His presence.

WORD FOR TODAY:

Psalm 27:8 KJV
[8] When thou saidst, Seek ye my face; my heart said unto thee, Thy face, Lord, will I seek.

SEPTEMBER 20

It's so funny how we think we know things, we think we know ourselves, and we are so very wrong. Only God is all knowing. We make plans and promises but not to follow through with them. Yes, we mean we will and are hopeful upon making them. But all too often that thing called "life" happens, and when we reflect back, so many things we intended, got extended, and we think we will do it later. That's why it's so important to inquire of the Lord and include the Holy Spirit in our every move. He already knows, so why not ask? Then you'll get fulfillment as opposed to disappointments.

WORD FOR TODAY:

Proverbs 20:24 KJV
[24] Man's goings are of the Lord; how can a man then understand his own way?

SEPTEMBER 21

So many times we expect God to show up through a big and extraordinary way, when He is just a small whisper in your heart if we are still long enough to listen and not just hear. Pray about everything and worry about nothing. God is in the solitude of your one-on-one relationship with Him. Allow Him to speak; slow down and don't get distracted by all the fiery darts and storms that come. Stop, pray, hear His voice, and believe. It's already done.

Word for Today:

1 Kings 19:12 KJV
[12] And after the earthquake a fire; but the Lord was not in the fire: and after the fire a still small voice.

September 22

Depending on your own strength and wisdom is fruitless, regardless of the effort you put into it. God is our source; without Him we can do nothing. He is our God, our Father, and our DNA is through him. It is Him who empowers us to keep moving forward, to pick up the pace and race toward the mark of a higher calling in Him. We seek not our own but His will for our lives. We must trust our Father to take very good care of us and to know that it is in Him we receive strength and joy to run the race of life that is set before us.

Word for Today:

Exodus 15:2 KJV
[2] The Lord is my strength and song, and he is become my salvation: he is my God, and I will prepare him an habitation; my father's God, and I will exalt him.

SEPTEMBER 23

Good is a God of love and forgiveness, and we must be, likewise, loving and forgiving. We are constantly committing sin, aware or unaware; either way, God forgives. Once we come into the light which is the knowledge of God's word and accept it, then we are one with Christ and one with His body (the people of God). So regardless of what someone does or says, we must forgive, not because they need it but because we need it. Forgiveness is freedom; we are then free from the burden of allowing someone else to control how we feel and our destination. When we are unforgiving, we are destined for a Christless eternity. That is something we don't want and work faithfully to prevent. Nothing and no one is worth you living in darkness and sin. It separates us from our Father, and that's no place we want to be.

Word for Today:

1 John 1:7-9 KJV
> [7] But if we walk in the light, as he is in the light, we have fellowship one with another, and the blood of Jesus Christ his Son cleanseth us from all sin. [8] If we say that we have no sin, we deceive ourselves, and the truth is not in us. [9] If we confess our sins, he is faithful and just to forgive us our sins, and to cleanse us from all unrighteousness.

September 24

Word for today:

Psalm 89:15-17 KJV

> [15] Blessed is the people that know the joyful sound: they shall walk, O Lord, in the light of thy countenance. [16] In thy name shall they rejoice all the day: and in thy righteousness shall they be exalted. [17] For thou art the glory of their strength: and in thy favour our horn shall be exalted.

September 25

If we seek to please man, that really means we fear man. What does it matter, how they feel about you? Man can only destroy the body, which is temporal; we should fear God above all else, who has the power to destroy both body and soul, which is everlasting. If we put more effort in trusting God, who is the source of everything you desire, you wouldn't have to fear what man can do to you. God, our Father, would never allow for anything bad to happen to us, without Him being glorified in and through it, and if God will get the glory, it's worth whatever you had to endure.

Word for today:

Proverbs 29:25 KJV

> [25] The fear of man bringeth a snare: but whoso putteth his trust in the Lord shall be safe.

September 26

Even when we mess up, God has made a way of escape for us to get it right. Adam messed up and couldn't redeem himself. Jesus came into the world through forty-two generations and redeemed us. He suffered, bled, and died just so we could be justified by faith in Him and never have to go to a Christless eternity. He continues to make a way of escape for us, knowing at some point we will get it. He sent our Comforter to keep us so that we will never see death and so we never have to be separated from Him. Thank God for life everlasting.

Word for Today:

1 Corinthians 15:21–22
> For since by man came death, by Man also came the resurrection of the dead. For as in Adam all die, even so in Christ all shall be made alive.

September 27

Where would we be, if it had not been for the Lord on our side? We would be in a world without hope. We would fail to strive and just merely survive. It is in God that we experience joy, peace, love, and kindness. We would be miserable with ourselves and with others. It's so good to know that when we are faced with challenges and obstacles in the road of life, that we have a Savior who is right there with us, carrying us through. He ensures that we will have a victorious outcome, much success, when we put our trust in Him.

Word for Today:

Psalm 27:13-14 KJV
> [13] I had fainted, unless I had believed to see the goodness of the Lord in the land of the living. [14] Wait on the Lord: be of good courage, and he shall strengthen thine heart: wait, I say, on the Lord.

September 28

You are saved, filled with God's Spirit and have Jesus right at your fingertips, and He knows all that you have been through and what you will go through. He knows exactly what it is like, so He understands what we feel, what we desire, what hurts, and what feels good. He understands because He was tempted just as we have been, and we can go boldly to Him for help because He can help you not to succumb to the temptation. He can hold you up and encourage you to see the bigger picture and not what's in front of you. He was without sin but understands your temptation and wants you to understand the enemy has nothing on you. God has already promised you that He would never leave you nor forsake you, He can't lie; now you must have the faith to believe it.

What are Some of Your Struggles, and What Keeps You in Doubt?

Word for Today:

Hebrews 4:14-16
> Seeing then that we have a great high priest, that is passed into the heavens, Jesus the Son of God, let us hold fast our profession. [15] For we have not an high priest which cannot be touched with the feeling of our infirmities; but was in all points tempted like as we are, yet without sin. [16] Let us therefore come boldly unto the throne of grace, that we may obtain mercy, and find grace to help in time of need.

September 29

Use your access card, the authority that we have through our elder brother and savior Jesus Christ. He is our mediator, our counselor. He stands waiting for us to call out to Him for help. Yes, He knows what we have need of before we ask, but He still wants to hear you ask. The word declares, "We have not because we ask not." The question is, why aren't we asking? A closed mouth will never get fed. Use your benefits in Christ; you have access to the throne of God, and it doesn't get any higher than that. You are connected not with just the right source, but the Source, so use it.

WORD FOR THE DAY:

Hebrews 4:14–16

Now that we know what we have—-Jesus, this great High Priest with ready access to God—-let's not let it slip through our fingers. We don't have a priest who is out of touch with our reality. He's been through weakness and testing, experienced it all—all but the sin. So let's walk right up to him and get what he is so ready to give. Take the mercy, accept the help

SEPTEMBER 30

When I think of God, all I can do is render praise unto Him. Every day He gives us brand-new mercies, His grace extends another day on earth. Here's the thing, He is not only with us here in the present but He walks with us right into eternity. That's why we should always give God glory in all things, acknowledging His will and what He allows. Every day, I ask Holy Spirit to quicken me when I make plans. I will acknowledge His power and will by saying, "If it's God's will, I will do this or that." Our lives are temporal in the earth, it's but a vapor of smoke that appears but for a moment and then vanishes. We need to prepare for eternity while in the present.

WORD FOR TODAY:

James 4:13–16 KJV

[13] Go to now, ye that say, To day or to morrow we will go into such a city, and continue there a year, and buy and sell,

and get gain: [14] Whereas ye know not what shall be on the morrow. For what is your life? It is even a vapour, that appeareth for a little time, and then vanisheth away. [15] For that ye ought to say, If the Lord will, we shall live, and do this, or that. [16] But now ye rejoice in your boastings: all such rejoicing is evil.

TAKE AWAYS (NOTES)

OCTOBER

Micah 5:12 KJV - [12] And I will cut off witchcrafts out of thine hand; and thou shalt have no more soothsayers.

October 1

God's word is yes and amen. He will never fall short of any of His promises to us. He will move heaven and earth to fulfil His word. We must believe every single word and stand firm on it. If He said it, that's it; you can count on Him to come through for you. Unlike so many of us, who say one thing and do something else, God is not like man, that He should lie. Believe Him and receive it.

Word for Today:

Isaiah 55:8–11 KJV

> [8] For my thoughts are not your thoughts, neither are your ways my ways, saith the Lord. [9] For as the heavens are higher than the earth, so are my ways higher than your ways, and my thoughts than your thoughts. [10] For as the rain cometh down, and the snow from heaven, and returneth not thither, but watereth the earth, and maketh it bring forth and bud, that it may give seed to

the sower, and bread to the eater: [11] So shall my word be that goeth forth out of my mouth: it shall not return unto me void, but it shall accomplish that which I please, and it shall prosper in the thing whereto I sent it.

OCTOBER 2

No one knows you better than God does — no one, no not even you. You aren't your own creation, you didn't give yourself life, and you don't even know when life will end and eternity began. As a matter of fact, you don't know what you will actually do the next minute. Though you may be a creature of habit and do everything routinely, anything can happen to throw you off your routine. God is the only one who is all knowing and knows you to an exact science. He chose you even before you were formed in the belly, so why keep ignoring Him? He is right here waiting for you to include Him in every area of your life, so don't even weigh the smallest matters without Him. He knows your ending from the beginning. He is your closest friend and without judgment.

WORD FOR TODAY:

Luke 12:7 KJV

[7] But even the very hairs of your head are all numbered. Fear not therefore: ye are of more value than many sparrows.

October 3

We are members of the body of Christ, whether legs, arms, eyes, nose, and so on. In other words, we are one body in Christ. He loves His body. He love us. We must trust Him in all things. Knowing that whatever is going on, He is in control and He will bring you out all right. Nothing just happens; God is the beginning and ending of your faith. He created us in His own image and knows exactly how much we can bare.

Word for Today:

Ephesians 5:30 KJV
>[30] For we are members of his body, of his flesh, and of his bones.

October 4

It's never about our power or might that we are able to withstand the evil of the day, but it's by the Holy Spirit. He is our strength and power; God has given Him to us for keeps. He knows what we need when we need it, and He steps in and performs miracles and victories on our behalf. We only need to include Him in our everyday decision making. He is our helper. We must do everything we can by the Spirit. Without His guidance, direction, and performance, we will fail every time.

Word for Today:

Zechariah 4:6 KJV

[6] Then he answered and spake unto me, saying, This is the word of the Lord unto Zerubbabel, saying, Not by might, nor by power, but by my spirit, saith the Lord of hosts.

October 5

No matter how difficult the day may seem or whatever problem arises, we must totally keep our eyes on God and know that He has already worked things out for your good. God should be our only source for life; in Him we should trust. If our food source is low, if we are homeless, if we have no friends, if we just look to God for our every need, He will fulfill it. There's nothing too hard for Him. He is in charge of everything, and He is the key to whatever you are dealing with. When we trust Him, we will have everlasting joy and peace, not fleeting happiness.

Word for Today:

Habakkuk 3:17-18 KJV

[17] Although the fig tree shall not blossom, neither shall fruit be in the vines; the labour of the olive shall fail, and the fields shall yield no meat; the flock shall be cut off from the fold, and there shall be no herd in the stalls: [18] Yet I will rejoice in the Lord, I will joy in the God of my salvation.

OCTOBER 6

We must bless and acknowledge God at all times and in all things, never getting weary in doing so. He knows just how much you can bear and is too great of a Father to put more on you. It's so important for us to stay close to Him, being connected at all times. Through the tough times, He's there; during the smooth days, He is there. He will never leave you nor forsake you. You should never be in a dark place; with Him there's light and life, beauty, and majesty.

WORD FOR TODAY:

Psalm 96:6 KJV
> [6] Honour and majesty are before him: strength and beauty are in his sanctuary.

Psalm 36:9 KJV
> [9] For with thee is the fountain of life: in thy light shall we see light.

OCTOBER 7

I will bless the Lord at all times, His praise will always be in my mouth. No matter what's going on, no matter how I feel, God will take care of me. I know that I have so much to be thankful for; even when things are down to the wire, God will work it out. I will not allow fear, anxiousness, people, or situations to deter or distort my focus. I will look unto the hills from where all my help comes from. I know that *all* my help comes from the Lord.

Word for Today:

1 Thessalonians 5:18 KJV

> [18] In every thing give thanks: for this is the will of God in Christ Jesus concerning you.

October 8

God loved us so much that He sent His Son to not only to die for us but in the process of going to the cross, did more for us in His short ministry than anyone could do in a lifetime. Jesus showed us how to live a righteous life, how to hold fast our faith, and how to be cool, calm, and collected in the face of adversity. He did it all out of obedience to the Father and love for us. There is no reason to falter under circumstances of life, knowing who our help comes from. Despite our many human frailties, He loves us and will never deny us our spiritual birthright, our covenant right given to us by the Father. There is no greater love than His.

Word for Today:

Jeremiah 31:3 KJV

> [3] The Lord hath appeared of old unto me, saying, Yea, I have loved thee with an everlasting love: therefore with lovingkindness have I drawn thee.

OCTOBER 9

I will bless the Lord no matter what the situation. I will not complain. Complaining is not acceptable in God's ears. He is the source of all things, and He is in the midst of everything related to us, so we must look to Him even when we don't understand circumstances. We must trust Him and not complain or be combative. Let's be still in his presence and know that God loves us and that there's nothing good He will withhold from you.

WORD FOR TODAY:

Philippians 2:14-15 KJV
   [14] Do all things without murmurings and disputings:
   [15] That ye may be blameless and harmless, the sons of God, without rebuke, in the midst of a crooked and perverse nation, among whom ye shine as lights in the world;

OCTOBER 10

We can live stress and worry free in this life if we only learn to trust God with everything. When we depend upon our own intellect and ability, we miss God, and we mess up. God is teaching us how we must totally and completely depend upon Him for all things. When we do that, we delight in Him and His ability to do anything but fail. We must always do good, never wavering from what is truth and right. You will never go wrong, and God will take complete care of you forever and always. Talk to Him about everything, and he shall bring it forth and present you in righteousness.

Word for Today:

Psalm 37:3-6 KJV

[3] Trust in the Lord, and do good; so shalt thou dwell in the land, and verily thou shalt be fed. [4] Delight thyself also in the Lord; and he shall give thee the desires of thine heart. [5] Commit thy way unto the Lord; trust also in him; and he shall bring it to pass. [6] And he shall bring forth thy righteousness as the light, and thy judgment as the noonday.

October 11

I can do nothing without God. He is the light that the shines my way. In each step I take, I depend on Him, not for just direction, but my strength is in Him. I cannot see the path ahead of me except He shows me and give me the strength to do so. I'm nothing without Him; He is the life I live and the air that gives me a freshness each day. He is the only solid and firm foundation to stand on. Only in Him do I put my trust at all times. I will cry out to Him my desires and concerns, for I know that He cares for me.

Word for Today:

Psalm 62:5-8 KJV

> [5] My soul, wait thou only upon God; for my expectation is from him. [6] He only is my rock and my salvation: he is my defence; I shall not be moved. [7] In God is my salvation and my glory: the rock of my strength, and my refuge, is in God. [8] Trust in him at all times; ye people, pour out your heart before him: God is a refuge for us. Selah.

October 12

Be real with God; in all that you do, be real. He knows your heart, mind, and soul. When worshipping Him, we must be real; it must be heartfelt and not ritualistic. It can't ever be something you do; it's who you are. When you think of His goodness toward you, it's an automatic response from the heart. We should not be overly consumed with what others think of us and our worship; we should only be concerned with what God knows about us and what's in our hearts. We must be real in whatever we say or do. God is the ultimate judge and will do according to our heart.

Word for Today:

John 4:23-24 KJV

> [23] But the hour cometh, and now is, when the true worshippers shall worship the Father in spirit and in truth: for the Father seeketh such to worship him. [24]

God is a Spirit: and they that worship him must worship him in spirit and in truth.

OCTOBER 13

The Lord will give you peace in the midst of your circumstances, if you be still and seek His presence. So many times we take matters into our own hands, feeling the need to be in control. God is in charge and has worked it out in your favor if you believe and ask in faith. Once you release it into His care, you can inhale His ability to do anything but fail, and exhale His peace which far exceeds your comprehension.

WORD FOR TODAY:

Psalm 46:10 KJV
[10] Be still, and know that I am God: I will be exalted among the heathen, I will be exalted in the earth.

OCTOBER 14

We must always do all things to the glory and honor of God because it is Him on the inside to will us and do. It is in Him that we are who we are and we do what we do; in us dwells no good thing. There is nothing good in my flesh; I can do nothing righteous, but by the Holy Spirit, I am the righteousness of God. It's Him on the inside, who b uses my vessel to perform the work. It is God, not me. We must be careful to not get puffed up by praise and accolades, God will reward us, so don't look for it from man. It's God doing the work through you. Make sure you let men and women know that it's not you but the God on the inside of you, our hope of glory.

WORD FOR TODAY:

1 Corinthians 15:10
> I labored more abundantly than they all, yet not I, but the grace of God which was with me.

OCTOBER 15

We have died and have been reincarnated in Christ Jesus. That person who didn't know God, no longer exists. We have been made over in the likeness of Christ and in the resurrection of His Spirit. We no longer do or say the things we did prior to submitting our life to Him. Sin no longer takes authority over us; sin actually smells foul in His nostrils and ours. No longer will we be associated with the unfruitful works of sin. We now live for Christ to bring others into the knowledge of the Kingdom of God. We are alive in Christ and will never die.

WORD FOR TODAY:

Galatians 2:20
> I have been crucified with Christ; it is no longer I who live, but Christ lives in me; and the life which I now live in the flesh I live by faith in the Son of God, who loved me and gave Himself for me.

John 11:26 KJV
> [26] And whosoever liveth and believeth in me shall never die. Believest thou this?

OCTOBER 16

In our most lonely or turbulent times of our lives, we tend to wallow in self-pity and feel worse. The good news is not that the loneliness or trouble won't last always, and the good news is that you are never alone. All you have to do is cast your cares on Him. He will take them. We suffer and struggle needlessly, simply because we neglect our constant companion. It's like having the answers to the test and not using them. We must know that God is with us and He can do exceedingly abundantly above anything we could imagine. There is nothing too hard for God; therefore, nothing is too hard for us. God is our comfort, and as we have come to depend and trust Him for all the answers, we must be a comfort and peace to others.

WORD FOR TODAY:

2 Corinthians 1:3–4 KJV
> [3] Blessed be God, even the Father of our Lord Jesus Christ, the Father of mercies, and the God of all comfort; [4] Who comforteth us in all our tribulation, that we may be able to comfort them which are in any trouble, by the comfort wherewith we ourselves are comforted of God.

OCTOBER 17

We spend countless hours worrying about things we can do nothing about. We feel that we can control situations or circumstances without understanding that we don't control anything. We do the things to prolong a good and healthy life but are a doctor's visit away from bad news. We must totally trust God in and for everything. Give Him honor and glory, knowing He is the master of your universe. He loves it when we give Him the love, honor, and respect due unto Him. When we lift our hands in sweet, holy surrender, God is right there to pick us up and hold us as He works things out for our good.

WORD FOR TODAY:

Luke 12:22-26 KJV

> [22] And he said unto his disciples, Therefore I say unto you, Take no thought for your life, what ye shall eat; neither for the body, what ye shall put on. [23] The life is more than meat, and the body is more than raiment. [24] Consider the ravens: for they neither sow nor reap; which neither have storehouse nor barn; and God feedeth them: how much more are ye better than the fowls? [25] And which of you with taking thought can add to his stature one cubit? [26] If ye then be not able to do that thing which is least, why take ye thought for the rest?

October 18

Be still and know that God's voice will lead and direct you. You should ignore anything outside of His voice; He will never lead you astray. Many times we get confused and will take a journey that takes us the long way home instead of following the path that God has chosen for us. Either way, there's a lesson to be learned. We must be attentive to God at all times and know that confusion is of the enemy. Any time you are unsure or things are not clear, don't forget to remember to inquire of God, and the path will be clear.

Word for Today:

John 10:14-15 KJV
> [14] I am the good shepherd, and know my sheep, and am known of mine. [15] As the Father knoweth me, even so know I the Father: and I lay down my life for the sheep.

October 19

Being real is the only requirement to freedom. We walk around masking what's really there in our hearts, minds, and souls. That causes us to be burden down and stressed. It's hard to feel real joy, love, and peace when everything is just a façade. God wants us to be real with Him as well as others and to be only concerned with what He knows about us, not how others view us. A liar will not tarry in His sight; He wants total honesty from us.

Word for Today:

1 John 1:7–10 KJV

[7] But if we walk in the light, as he is in the light, we have fellowship one with another, and the blood of Jesus Christ his Son cleanseth us from all sin. [8] If we say that we have no sin, we deceive ourselves, and the truth is not in us. [9] If we confess our sins, he is faithful and just to forgive us our sins, and to cleanse us from all unrighteousness. [10] If we say that we have not sinned, we make him a liar, and his word is not in us.

October 20

For we shall know the truth and the truth shall make us free. That's God's word to us—it's strong, confident, and right! If you know God, you know all truth. He will never allow His children to be taken in or down by lies. We can only have abundant life in this world when we know what truth is. The truth is, God has created me and you in His image. We are beautiful creatures in and through Him only. It's not just skin deep; it's all the way through the heart, and no matter how others may see you or say about you, you know the truth. You are a beautiful person in Christ.

Word for Today:

Psalm 139:14 KJV

[14] I will praise thee; for I am fearfully and wonderfully made: marvellous are thy works; and that my soul knoweth right well.

October 21

As long as we are in this body, we will all be tempted to sin. God never said that we wouldn't be. What He did say is that He would never tempt us and that we are tempted by our own sin and enticed. We must give our weaknesses to Him, and He will graciously take them. We cannot fight the sin disease on our own; we need Holy Spirit to keep us and to convict us when we step outside of God's will, even for a moment. That's why it was so important that Jesus sent the Holy Spirit to dwell on the inside of us. While Jesus was on the earth, He kept the disciples, but He knew just as soon as He left, they wouldn't have the ability to refrain from Satan's sinful tactics. We can deny it all day long, but God knows our struggle. He knows our name and every weight and the sin that so easily overtakes us. All things are naked and open before Him, so release your stronghold to Him and be delivered and set free from the yoke of sin bondage. Sin isn't worth being separated from our God.

Word for today:

Galatians 5:19
> The works of the flesh are evident, which are: adultery, fornication, uncleanness, lewdness.

Hebrews 4:13 KJV
> [13] Neither is there any creature that is not manifest in his sight: but all things are naked and opened unto the eyes of him with whom we have to do.

October 22

I will look unto the hills from which comes all of my help, knowing my help comes from God above. No matter the circumstances God is in control, I will not fear people or circumstances, knowing this too shall pass. I will trust God no matter what.

Word for today:

Psalm 21:6 KJV
> [6] For thou hast made him most blessed for ever: thou hast made him exceeding glad with thy countenance.

October 23

Jesus is the way, He is the truth, and there's life everlasting in Him. When we can shut off the world and read the word, we find joy, peace, and calm. We get in Him, He is in us, and we cannot be downtrodden with depression and the pressures of this life. We see with a new set of eyes, our minds get renewed, and our bodies strengthened physically and spiritually. Stay in Christ as He is in God, His Holy Spirit dwells within us, and we all are one.

Word for Today:

John 17:20-23 KJV

> [20] Neither pray I for these alone, but for them also which shall believe on me through their word; [21] That they all may be one; as thou, Father, art in me, and I in thee, that they also may be one in us: that the world may believe that thou hast sent me. [22] And the glory which thou gavest me I have given them; that they may be one, even as we are one: [23] I in them, and thou in me, that they may be made perfect in one; and that the world may know that thou hast sent me, and hast loved them, as thou hast loved me.

October 24

Push away from the dinner table and pray. That is the phrase the Holy Spirit kept speaking to me. So many times it's hard for us to hear from God or get results because we won't fast and pray. I remember the apostles asking Jesus why they couldn't cast demons out of the boy, and Jesus simply responded that it comes out through by fasting and prayer. Some struggles we pray and pray for but get no release. God is saying if you are truly wanting results, push away and pray. Show God you are passionate and serious about your petition by afflicting your body with the lack of enjoyable food and cry out from your heart. God searches and knows the heart. For out of it flows the rivers of life.

WORD FOR TODAY:

Joel 2:12
> [12] "Now, therefore," says the LORD, "Turn to Me with all your heart, With fasting, with weeping, and with mourning."

Psalm 44:21 KJV
> [21] Shall not God search this out? for he knoweth the secrets of the heart.

OCTOBER 25

Ever heard the phrase, "a closed mouth won't get fed"? It holds true with our praise and thankful heart as well. God wants to hear our praise, our acknowledgment of who He is in our lives and how great He has been to us. Let's open our mouth wide in expectancy, for God will fill it with the spiritual fruit of His word and give you the desires of your heart as you cry out to Him in obedience.

WORD FOR TODAY:

Psalm 81:10
> [10] I am the LORD your God, who brought you out of the land of Egypt; open your mouth wide, and I will fill it.

OCTOBER 26

We are one, inseparable, and together. There is no way to separate from oneself, there's no way to separate yourself from our Creator, and we are one. He is in us as we are in Him, and nothing or no one can take us out of Him. The one thing we can be sure of is our oneness in Christ. We are never alone and should never go at anything without Him. Let's engage Him (the Triune God) in everything. Remember He is in us from the beginning to the end throughout all eternity.

WORD FOR TODAY:

John 15:5 KJV
> [5] I am the vine, ye are the branches: He that abideth in me, and I in him, the same bringeth forth much fruit: for without me ye can do nothing.

OCTOBER 27

God is a consuming fire, it is He who gets rid of everything that is bad, once you give it to Him. Release those things in your life that keeps you bound, keeps you from growing spiritually.

You do not have the strength of power to do it by yourself. You need God's spirit on the inside of you to give you the strength to give up everything that is not pleasing to Him. Your desire is to please God in everything that you do and in all that you say. The more you draw close to Him the more you'll want to give up those things that opposes His character and His desire for you. Draw closer to Him by reading His word, talking to Him as friend with friend. He will lead and guide you unto all truth and righteous behavior.

WORD FOR TODAY:

Deuteronomy 4:23
> [23]Be careful not to forget the covenant of the Lord your God that he made with you; do not make for yourselves an idol in the form of anything the Lord your God has forbidden. 24For the Lord your God is a consuming fire, a jealous God.

OCTOBER 28

Could you even imagine not being able to hear God's word? It's vital for us to give close attention to reading, exhortation, and doctrine. God's word is the light that brightens our path. We can't move or live without God's word. It is food for our soul. Our souls suffer from spiritual malnutrition when we fail to feast off of the word of God. We feed that natural, fleshly man so that it gets as plump as it wants to be, but that spirit man, the inward parts that will last forever, is being neglected food for the spiritual soul. Thereby, we stumble and fall because we are deprived nourishment of God's word. Remember to feed your spirit man; that's what's eternal. Know the word of God. It's our weapon against the enemy. Remember it's exactly what Jesus used against the enemy when he tried Him in the wilderness. Thank God for His food.

Word for Today:

Amos 8:11

> [11] "Behold, the days are coming," says the Lord GOD, "that I will send a famine on the land, not a famine of bread, nor a thirst for water, but of hearing the words of the LORD.

October 29

We are the work of the Lord, created expressly by Him and of Him. We must know that we are examples of His holiness, majesty, and perfectness. As such, we must do good deeds because everything God did,

made, created, and will do is very good. Our actions should display His attributes. His Spirit and our spirit are united, and we cannot do anything without Him. In all we do, we must give God all glory, honor, and praise.

WORD FOR TODAY:

Ephesians 2:10 KJV

[10] For we are his workmanship, created in Christ Jesus unto good works, which God hath before ordained that we should walk in them.

OCTOBER 30

It seems when there's contention, strife, confusion, it's hard to feel God's' presence or even to hear His voice. Get in a quiet place and space within and call to Him immediately. He will answer, and you will hear His voice because you have blocked out the enemy. Confusion is of the devil, and God has no place in it, so you must step back and into His presence. Getting in His presence simply means reading His word and praying to Him. We are spiritual beings, having a natural experience. We get caught up into the natural, the secular, and neglect that which is spiritual and eternal. Don't get caught up into the enemy's devices; always know that God is with you always, and nothing or no one can take you away from Him. Call to Him at all times.

WORD FOR TODAY:

John 10:27-28 KJV

[27] My sheep hear my voice, and I know them, and they follow me: [28] And I give unto them eternal life; and they shall never perish, neither shall any man pluck them out of my hand.

October 31

God has placed His spirit within us so that we might be like Him. He has given us His Spirit to keep, lead, and direct us. Everything that we do and all that we say should be through the unction of the Holy Spirit. We must know that God is not just with is but in us, and at any time we can call upon Him and He has to come through for us. We have a more sure salvation than them of old because we have the Holy Spirit within us. We no longer have to fall prey to the enemy's devices. We are a vessel to be used by God and God only.

Word for Today:

1 Corinthians 6:19-20 KJV

> [19] What? know ye not that your body is the temple of the Holy Ghost which is in you, which ye have of God, and ye are not your own? [20] For ye are bought with a price: therefore glorify God in your body, and in your spirit, which are God's.

TAKE AWAYS (NOTES)

NOVEMBER

Psalm 9:1 KJV - [1] I will praise thee, O Lord, with my whole heart; I will shew forth all thy marvellous works.

NOVEMBER 1

I need you now, O God. My faith is strong. I know you are with us, and I know our lives are in your hands. Lord, I believe you are turning sickness around and destroying it to prove your word to us. I know you felt and had experienced the same things we have endured and more. You suffered and died for us. I wasn't the one sent from judgment hall to judgment hall. You were, and you did it all for me. You said by your stripes we are healed. So I come boldly, believing, as I ask you to heal miraculously from any sickness or disease that tries to trespass on your vessel. We know the medicine is extracted from various herbs you have created, and for that we thank you. We thank you for machines and equipment that now help to sustain life, knowing that it's your grace and mercy. Heal, deliver, and set free *all* diseases and infirmities in the body of your people. We know it's not your will that any should be sick. We declare and decree as David did in Psalm 103:3. It is done; we believe and receive healing of autoimmune diseases, diabetes, hypertension, liver damage, bone density decline, heart disease, depression, oppression, demonic attacks, and emotional distress. We bind up witchcraft and sorcery in the name of Jesus. We speak good health and wealth to be about Kingdom business. We know that everything works out in the end for our good. It is so, in Jesus' name and by His stripes we are healed.

WORD FOR TODAY:

Hebrews 4:14-16 KJV

[14] Seeing then that we have a great high priest, that is passed into the heavens, Jesus the Son of God, let us hold fast our profession. [15] For we have not an high priest which cannot be touched with the feeling of our infirmities; but was in all points tempted like as we are, yet without sin. [16] Let us therefore come boldly unto the throne of grace, that we may obtain mercy, and find grace to help in time of need.

Romans 8:28-29 KJV

[28] And we know that all things work together for good to them that love God, to them who are the called according to his purpose. [29] For whom he did foreknow, he also did predestinate to be conformed to the image of his Son, that he might be the firstborn among many brethren.

NOVEMBER 2

WORD FOR TODAY:

Isaiah 30:15 KJV
   [15] For thus saith the Lord God, the holy One of Israel; In returning and rest shall ye be saved; in quietness and in confidence shall be your strength: and ye would not.

Psalm 116:5-7 KJV
   [5] Gracious is the Lord, and righteous; yea, our God is merciful. [6] The Lord preserveth the simple: I was brought low, and he helped me. [7] Return unto thy rest, O my soul; for the Lord hath dealt bountifully with thee.

NOVEMBER 3

Everything has a purpose; nothing just happens. These are things I've come to find to be true. We must know that everything attained in this life is never to be compared to what will be attained in heaven, in the eternity that is to come. Be determined as Paul, knowing that everything I have and ever desire to be is in Christ; everything I have is God and if it is gone, it's gone. It was meant to be. Totally depend on God and no one else or nothing else. God is what matters, and when we seek to please Him, everything else will fall into place.

Word for Today:

Philippians 3:7-8 KJV

> [7] But what things were gain to me, those I counted loss for Christ. [8] Yea doubtless, and I count all things but loss for the excellency of the knowledge of Christ Jesus my Lord: for whom I have suffered the loss of all things, and do count them but dung, that I may win Christ,

November 4

Is it pleasing unto you, Lord? Am I pleasing unto you? If you ever want to know whether you are doing the right thing, making the right decision, or saying the right things, simply ask Him. He makes us perfect in every *good* work. If it's not to edify, it's not God. He is a God of peace and not confusion neither turmoil. That's why the world had to come into order of perfection, He spoke to it, and it did exactly what was commanded. When God speaks, we must obey. Don't forget we are spiritual beings having a natural experience. How do you know what to do, if you should do this or that? Stop going at it alone and ask our Creator, He has all the *right* answers for you to do good.

Word for Today:

Hebrews 13:20-21 KJV

> [20] Now the God of peace, that brought again from the dead our Lord Jesus, that great shepherd of the

sheep, through the blood of the everlasting covenant, [21] Make you perfect in every good work to do his will, working in you that which is well pleasing in his sight, through Jesus Christ; to whom be glory for ever and ever. Amen.

NOVEMBER 5

God has given us many promises, and the one that we most often forget is that He is always with us. Even when we disconnect from Him, which we often do in times of trouble, when we fall prey to sin, or during the times of mishap. But God is always there, He's only waiting for you to acknowledge His presence and invite Him into your circumstances. He already knew what you would encounter, but at some point He wants us to recognize that in all things we must look to Him and trust that He will bring us through. He will never leave us nor forsake us. He is always with us; don't ever forget it. He wrote the ending, and His promises are always yes and amen.

WORD FOR TODAY:

Genesis 28:15 KJV
[15] And, behold, I am with thee, and will keep thee in all places whither thou goest, and will bring thee again into this land; for I will not leave thee, until I have done that which I have spoken to thee of.

November 6

We have this thing called life all wrong. It's not about us. When we come to understand that it's all about God, then we will get the results desired. We must seek to please Him every waking moment and commune with Him. Never go at it alone, even when you think you can. Engage Him in your walk. You think you know, but He actually knows. He wrote and commissioned you and all that pertains to you.

When you diligently seek Him, delight, praise, and worship, then He will give you what is in your heart. Stop complaining or being slothful; be about His business, and I promise you'll get your desires met.

Word for Today:

John 8:29 KJV
> [29] And he that sent me is with me: the Father hath not left me alone; for I do always those things that please him.

Psalm 37:4 KJV
> [4] Delight thyself also in the Lord; and he shall give thee the desires of thine heart.

November 7

Our desires should be to please God first and foremost, knowing that our lives are in His hands and He will keep that which we have committed unto Him. We have committed our lives unto the Lord, so all that we encounter in life is to His glory and to His honor. He loves us and knows what is best for us. Therefore, whatever the situation is, inquire of the Lord. He will answer speedily. Understand that He is ours, and we are His, and without Him, we can do nothing. There's beauty in knowing Him and being in Him. We see things through His eyes, and everything He has made is beautiful. Even when we go through things, the beauty is knowing that all will end well. Place everything in His hands, and you will get beautiful results.

WORD FOR TODAY:

Psalm 27:4 KJV
> [4] One thing have I desired of the Lord, that will I seek after; that I may dwell in the house of the Lord all the days of my life, to behold the beauty of the Lord, and to enquire in his temple.

NOVEMBER 8

The Lord God is all we need. So many times we fear saying that because, of course, we need people in our lives. However, when you have God, He brings the right people into your life and remove the ones who shouldn't be there. We must know that there's no mountain too high, no valley too low, neither giant too big; when God is with us, we have nothing to fear. He is our protector, guide, and deliverer. He will never let go of our hand. We can do all things through Him, and without Him we can do nothing. He is our life.

Word for Today:

Isaiah 41:10 KJV
> [10] Fear thou not; for I am with thee: be not dismayed; for I am thy God: I will strengthen thee; yea, I will help thee; yea, I will uphold thee with the right hand of my righteousness.

November 9

There is no need to worry or fret about the future, for God is with us in the future. Worries and fears are just more darts the enemy throws our way to distort our view or cause us to stray from the kingdom. God will take care of all of us, so why worry about uncertainties of life when we have a certain God who is able to keep us? Be strong in the Lord and excited because there are only great things in store.

Word for Today:

Deuteronomy 31:6 KJV
> [6] Be strong and of a good courage, fear not, nor be afraid of them: for the Lord thy God, he it is that doth go with thee; he will not fail thee, nor forsake thee.

NOVEMBER 10

Not I, but the Christ lives inside of me, and it is He that empowers me to do, to have, and to be. He will keep that which I have committed unto Him. We have committed ourselves to Him, spiritually and physically, and He has promised to keep us. Never think that you are alone in any situation and never make a permanent decision on a temporary situation. There's always a solution. Never quit, never give up, endure until the end, and allow God to move in and through you. Step out of the way while He makes a way, and you'll come out victorious every time.

WORD FOR TODAY:

Jude 1:24-25 KJV
    [24] Now unto him that is able to keep you from falling, and to present you faultless before the presence of his glory with exceeding joy, [25] To the only wise God our Saviour, be glory and majesty, dominion and power, both now and ever. Amen.

NOVEMBER 11

Don't forget to reflect on the wonderful, marvelous things God has done. Commune with Him all throughout the day. There's no mountain too high with Him. We must know our strength lies in Him. Otherwise, we fail when we go at it alone. Seek God for everything. He already knows your tomorrow, so why not trust Him with it and in it? He truly knows how much we can bear. He has given us the right challenges at the right time, and they are precisely what His will is, when we walk, talk, and live in Him.

WORD FOR TODAY:

Psalm 105:4-5 KJV
   [4] Seek the Lord, and his strength: seek his face evermore. [5] Remember his marvellous works that he hath done; his wonders, and the judgments of his mouth;

NOVEMBER 12

It really makes you feel good when you do something for someone and they take the time to write you a thank you note or just simply say thank you and let you know how much your act of kindness means to them. God wants a thank you, a grateful heart, the whispers of love and appreciation as much as we do. Everyday is a day of thanksgiving, with each gift that God gives us, thanksgiving should just roll off of our lips so naturally. The gift of lift is one that we see each day, food, clothes, a place to sleep, the list goes on and on. Lets remember to give God thanks throughout this day and everyday. Open and close each day with thanksgiving on your lips.

Word for Today:

Psalm 100:4 KJV

[4] Enter into his gates with thanksgiving, and into his courts with praise: be thankful unto him, and bless his name.

November 13

I still have joy. It's not a fleeting emotion or a feeling I get sometimes. I have the joy of the Holy Spirit on the inside, and no matter what happens, God gives me the peace and joy of His presence. I know this trouble shall pass. He is my joy. No man, woman, boy, or girl can give me the joy that comes with knowing God intimately. I have His Spirit, dwelling on the inside. I still have joy.

Word for Today:

Romans 15:13 KJV

[13] Now the God of hope fill you with all joy and peace in believing, that ye may abound in hope, through the power of the Holy Ghost.

November 14

It's all right that you don't fit in with the world. You are different, so dare to be different. When we are younger, it's really a struggle because we don't quite understand why we don't look like our peers, talk like them, or even act the way they do.

Then we mature and realize we are chosen to hold up a standard of holiness. New converts sometimes struggle with loneliness because their walk with Christ brings a separation. Those old friends are no longer interested in you, and nothing you do seem to feel right when you are with them. It's because you are chosen, you are of a royal priesthood, and you are kings and queens in God's family. Praise God for not just calling us out of sin and darkness but bringing us into His marvelous light so that we might be a light to others. So, it's okay to be different; our elder brother Jesus was also different. When we understand who we are and whose we are, we realize with much joy and praise that we are adopted into a royal family in the Kingdom of God. What an honor to have.

Word for Today:

1 Peter 2:9 KJV

> [9] But ye are a chosen generation, a royal priesthood, an holy nation, a peculiar people; that ye should shew forth the praises of him who hath called you out of darkness into his marvellous light:

November 15

Yes we can; because Jesus did, we can. He paid it all and gave the ultimate price so that we won't have to. No matter what you are dealing with, take a moment to step back and step to God. Think of all the goodness He has bestowed upon you. Then you'll begin to replace worry with joy. His peace will overtake you as you begin to praise and worship Him.

WORD FOR TODAY:

John 16:33 KJV

[33] These things I have spoken unto you, that in me ye might have peace. In the world ye shall have tribulation: but be of good cheer; I have overcome the world.

NOVEMBER 16

We are *not* in a losing battle. God is with us. He is for us and will be with us in all that we do or go through in life and eternity to follow. We should not be dismayed or shaken when things come our way. We must embrace the journey and know that God is leading the way. We can do all things in and through Him. He continually carries us when we can no longer walk on our own. He continues to guide us when we can't find our way. He holds us up when we feel weak. He speaks blessings and life when we are feeling depressed or when the stresses of life gets to us. He simply ask that we cast our cares on Him for He cares for us. He doesn't want us to suffer needlessly. He can handle all our burdens, but we must know there's a blessing if we learn the lesson.

WORD FOR TODAY:

Psalm 73:23–26 KJV

[23] Nevertheless I am continually with thee: thou hast holden me by my right hand. [24] Thou shalt guide me with thy counsel, and afterward receive me to glory. [25] Whom have I in heaven but thee? and there is none

upon earth that I desire beside thee. [26] My flesh and my heart faileth: but God is the strength of my heart, and my portion for ever.

NOVEMBER 17

When we are in Christ, He is our hope, strength, and determination. We are His righteousness, and there's no condemnation for us as we walk as He has walked. As we follow His lead, there's no way to stray. He keeps us on that straight and narrow pathway and keeps us righteous. We are no longer condemned by the deeds of the flesh, but we are the very righteousness of God.

WORD FOR TODAY:

Romans 8:1-2 KJV
[1] There is therefore now no condemnation to them which are in Christ Jesus, who walk not after the flesh, but after the Spirit. [2] For the law of the Spirit of life in Christ Jesus hath made me free from the law of sin and death.

NOVEMBER 18

We must go to God with and for everything, He is the ultimate source of everything in life and in eternity. We know nothing in and of ourselves. We can only speculate, plan, or anticipate outcomes, but God only knows. We must pray specifically, believe, and begin thanking God. Every day believe, even when the doubts or disbelief enter in. Just go to God about that and ask Him to help your unbelief. He is the way for all sufficiency. Trust and never doubt that He can do anything and everything but fail. And when you know that, you know that our all-powerful, all-knowing God can and will take care of all that concerns you, you can rest in His peace.

Word for Today:

Philippians 4:6–7 KJV
> [6] Be careful for nothing; but in every thing by prayer and supplication with thanksgiving let your requests be made known unto God. [7] And the peace of God, which passeth all understanding, shall keep your hearts and minds through Christ Jesus.

November 19

We don't have to worry or allow things to make us afraid. God knows that we are His, and He will be right by our side. He will not let any evil befall us. He is constant in ridding us of whatever comes our way. Where we are weak, He is strong. Trust Him in the rain just as you do in the sun, in the valley as you do the mountaintop. God is faithful and true. God will always see us through, even throughout eternity.

He will never leave us.

Word for Today:

Exodus 15:13 KJV
> [13] Thou in thy mercy hast led forth the people which thou hast redeemed: thou hast guided them in thy strength unto thy holy habitation.

November 20

How amazing the grace of God is toward us. He loves us despite us. So many times we work hard doing ministry and helping others, not because it's who we are, but because it's something to do for accolades. Our busy work here will not earn us a place in heaven. We are busy doing God's work because it's in us; His spirit is in us, so we are Christlike and only want Him to be pleased with us. If we are doing it for any other reason, God does not acknowledge it. If you expect your reward from man, don't expect it from God. Our motives have to be true and from a sincere heart because God looks at and judges the heart.

Word for Today:

Ephesians 2:8-9 KJV
> [8] For by grace are ye saved through faith; and that not of yourselves: it is the gift of God: [9] Not of works, lest any man should boast.

Psalm 62:8 KJV
> [8] Trust in him at all times; ye people, pour out your heart before him: God is a refuge for us. Selah.

NOVEMBER 21

God is always with us, and He is our peace. Knowing and believing His promises, we should constantly give God praise. He loves getting praise just like we do. He can never get enough of us fussing over Him. Every day live in God's peace, knowing He is always present. That too shall keep us doing the right thing.

WORD FOR TODAY:

Luke 24:36 KJV
> [36] And as they thus spake, Jesus himself stood in the midst of them, and saith unto them, Peace be unto you.

Matthew 28:20 KJV
> [20] Teaching them to observe all things whatsoever I have commanded you: and, lo, I am with you alway, even unto the end of the world. Amen.

Hebrews 13:15 KJV
> [15] By him therefore let us offer the sacrifice of praise to God continually, that is, the fruit of our lips giving thanks to his name.

November 22

Never neglect to tell of God's goodness and to sing of His praise. When we rise in the morning, all through the day and as we retire for the night, give God praise, thanking Him for all that He has done, what He is doing, and what He will do in the future. God didn't have to do "it", whatever "it" is, and if you are reading this, I know you can think of a whole lot of "its" that our God has done for you. Protecting you from dangers that you see and the ones you don't. Taking care of your needs, your loved ones needs, provider shelter, employment, health and strength, etc…. As believers, we must testify of His goodness so that others may hear and rejoice in our Savior alone. Remember, we overcome the enemy by the blood of the Lamb, and by the **word** of our **testimony**;

Word for Today:

Psalm 26:7 KJV
   [7] That I may publish with the voice of thanksgiving, and tell of all thy wondrous works.

Psalm 26:12
   In the congregations I will bless the LORD.

November 23

What could come between you and the peace of God? What will stand between you and eternal life with God? In other

NOVEMBER

words, what could possibly be more important than your relationship with God?

Nothing in this world is worth losing eternal life with Christ. No amount of money, no relationships, whether good, bad or indifferent, no emotional distress, no houses or land, nothing is more important. Don't allow temporary situations keep you from a permanent relationship and oneness with our Lord. It's so not worth it.

WORD FOR TODAY:

Romans 8:38-39 KJV
> [38] For I am persuaded, that neither death, nor life, nor angels, nor principalities, nor powers, nor things present, nor things to come, [39] Nor height, nor depth, nor any other creature, shall be able to separate us from the love of God, which is in Christ Jesus our Lord.

NOVEMBER 24

Everything living yields praises to God involuntarily but man. He is our joy and our salvation; everything is in Him. How can we go day by day without giving Him praise and thanks for all He has done? Even the elements and nature sing of His praises. The stars of heaven dance in joy for His goodness. When we think of the goodness of our God, our souls can't help but cry out, "Thank you, Lord. You are mighty and true, full of love, patient and long suffering. You are worthy to be praised. From the rising of the sun to the going down of the same, you are worthy!"

Word for Today:

Psalm 89:5 KJV
 [5] And the heavens shall praise thy wonders, O Lord: thy faithfulness also in the congregation of the saints.

November 25

It's God who gives us hope and lets us know through His Holy Spirit that everything will be all right. We can choose to look past our circumstances and see as He sees. We can't lose with God. His promises are clear and concise, and He works everything out for our good as Roman 8:28 states. We must give Him thanks and praise for all He is to us and what He will be in the future. Trust Him to do the impossible.

Word for Today:

Romans 15:13 KJV
 [13] Now the God of hope fill you with all joy and peace in believing, that ye may abound in hope, through the power of the Holy Ghost.

November 26

Every day should be a day of thanksgiving. Thank God, not only when you pray in the morning or before you end the day, but also throughout the day. In the good, give Him thanks; and even in the not so good, give Him thanks. Give God thanks when you are well and when you are sick, and when you are blessed and when you are distressed, knowing that all things will work out for our good. God loves it when we give Him praise. He delights in our giving Him thanks.

When we give God thanks in all things at all times, we are acknowledging His Lordship over our lives, as well as His pre-eminence, His power, and His love for us. As we give Him continual thanks, He will continue to rain down blessings upon us. When we give Him thanks in the midst of our trials, it

minimizes our view of the trials. We stop looking at the problem and look unto the hills from whence cometh all of our help. Our help comes from the Lord Almighty, who is all powerful and all knowing. You are actually releasing it into the almighty hands of God. I encourage you to give Him thanks in everything and at all times and see just how great things will work out. Try God without any doubt, and know He will work it out.

WORD FOR THE DAY:

Psalm 118:24 KJV
> [24] This is the day which the Lord hath made; we will rejoice and be glad in it.

Psalm 116:17–19 KJV
> [17] I will offer to thee the sacrifice of thanksgiving, and will call upon the name of the Lord. [18] I will pay my vows unto the Lord now in the presence of all his people, [19] In the courts of the Lord's house, in the midst of thee, O Jerusalem. Praise ye the Lord.

NOVEMBER 27

God has called us to peace at all times. Jesus was a great example of how we should behave in the peace that God gave us when He created us in His image. God's peace should rule in our lives even when the enemy tries to take our peace by referring to our peace as cowardly, so don't be dismayed. He just wants to get a rise out of you. He's not worth you losing your peace. Stand still and speak peace and give God praise because His peace rules in our lives.

WORD FOR TODAY:

Colossians 3:15 KJV
[15] And let the peace of God rule in your hearts, to the which also ye are called in one body; and be ye thankful.

NOVEMBER 28

All God wants is our praise for the wondrous things He has done and continues to do in our lives. Acknowledging the fact of His sovereignty is high on His list. He already knows He can do anything but fail, and He wants us to realize there's no failure in Him. He can do what no other doctors, lawyers, spouses, or employers can do. We must be totally dependent upon Him and never cease to give Him praise. David said if he had the tongues of a thousand, it still wouldn't be enough to give Him the praises that He deserves. Praise God with all that is within you: your mouth, your feet and hands, and even the instruments. When I look at nature, I realize even the flowers and trees lift their hands in praise. Let's give God praise at all times; don't let it always be a sacrifice. He loves us so much that He doesn't even want us to stress, He told us to cast our cares on Him for He cares for us. There was an old hymn that says, "Oh what needless pains we bear all because we do not carry everything to God in prayer." Do not stress because we are blessed. *Give it to God.* He alone can bear our struggles so that we don't have to.

Psalm 107:21-22 KJV

[21] Oh that men would praise the Lord for his goodness, and for his wonderful works to the children of men! [22] And let them sacrifice the sacrifices of thanksgiving, and declare his works with rejoicing.

WORD FOR TODAY:

1 Peter 5:6-7 KJV

[6] Humble yourselves therefore under the mighty hand of God, that he may exalt you in due time: [7] Casting all your care upon him; for he careth for you.

NOVEMBER 29

We must seek to please God and not man, and trust the plan that he has for you. Stop trying to figure it out. Look to God; He has worked it out. God who knows the ending from the beginning, has it all worked out and guess what? He's working it in your favor.

SCENT OF HEAVEN

WORD FOR TODAY:

Psalm 32:8 KJV

[8] I will instruct thee and teach thee in the way which thou shalt go: I will guide thee with mine eye.

NOVEMBER 30

There's no need to worry or fret. God said He will satisfy our soul.. His grace and mercy toward us is everlasting. During the time of recession, God provided, never missing a beat. The righteous will always fair well. We must hold God to His promises to take care of all our needs. There's no recession in the Kingdom of God; there's no lack and absolutely no denial. Our access card works even better when the world is on a decline because God wants to show us that it's not about what man will say or do; it's not about the economy or systems failing. It's all about Him. As we put our trust in Him, He will make our impossible way possible.

WORD FOR TODAY:

Isaiah 58:11 KJV

[11] And the Lord shall guide thee continually, and satisfy thy soul in drought, and make fat thy bones:

and thou shalt be like a watered garden, and like a spring of water, whose waters fail not.

TAKE AWAYS (NOTES)

DECEMBER

Matthew 1:21 KJV - [21] And she shall bring forth a son, and thou shalt call his name JESUS: for he shall save his people from their sins.

December 1

If you don't have a plan in place, you are liable to repeat this year's folly next year. Lessons not learned are repeated. Nothing will come out when something is out of order. You can't expect to prosper and cheat on our tithe.

Even though you had an awesome year, don't repeat it; exceed it. Start to set your goals and vision for you and your family. Began to speak what you desire to see them happen next year. Include God in your vision; we should do absolutely nothing without Him. It's imperative that you set spiritual goals as well as the physical and financial goals. What we do for Christ will last throughout eternity. We shall be rewarded for our acts of kindness, for speaking the good news, and for all we do for God's kingdom. Your temple is God's dwelling place; seek Him for His will for His temple.

Word for Today:

Romans 12:1-3 (KJV)
 I beseech you therefore, brethren, by the mercies of God, that ye present your bodies a living sacrifice, holy, acceptable unto God, which is your reasonable service. [2] And be not conformed to this world: but be ye transformed by the renewing of your mind, that ye may prove what is that good, and acceptable, and perfect, will of God. [3] For I say, through the grace given unto me, to every man that is among you, not to think of himself more highly than he ought to think; but to think soberly, according as God hath dealt to every man the measure of faith.

December 2

I will trust and wait only on the Lord for He has given me peace. I know that He will deliver me out of all my troubles and heal me from every affliction of my body. I am one with Him. There's no sickness or diseases within Him, so I will not give way to sickness or disease. I know this too shall pass. God has delivered and healed me. I will walk in it and wait patiently on my Lord who can do more than I have ever imagined or dreamed.

WORD FOR TODAY:

Jeremiah 31:3 KJV

[3] The Lord hath appeared of old unto me, saying, Yea, I have loved thee with an everlasting love: therefore with lovingkindness have I drawn thee.

DECEMBER 3

We must realize every attack is a spiritual attack. There is no such thing as happenstance. The enemy is out to kill, steal, and destroy. That's reality, and we must know the power of God that is within us. We must fight the good fight of faith, keeping on the whole armor of God. We can never release our armor; if we do, we are open season for the enemy to take us out. Even when the battle is too strong, Jesus is there, and all we need to do is ask Him for help. We are spiritual beings having a natural experience.

WORD FOR TODAY:

Ephesians 6:12 KJV

[12] For we wrestle not against flesh and blood, but against principalities, against powers, against the rulers of the darkness of this world, against spiritual wickedness in high places.

December 4

his study is so timely, Lord, after I just wrote the same things to my siblings asking them to focus on you, Lord. We have enough battles going on in the spirit realm; there's no time to find things to fight about among ourselves. I know that situations come to take me away from you. I will see you in everything and give it to you; it's far more than I can handle or bear. Continue to keep me in perfect peace as I keep my mind stayed on you. I have to be a lively stone, an effective witness of your goodness and everlasting mercy. Man will surely point out all our faults and the sins of our past, but I'm thankful, God, that you are a God who forgives, and judgment is in your hands only. Thank you for brand-new mercies, even for the mercy you have for the whole world.

Words for the Day:

Ephesians 6:12 (KJV)
> For we wrestle not against flesh and blood, but against principalities, against powers, against the rulers of the darkness of this world, against spiritual wickedness in high places.

December 5

So many times we get caught up in what others are saying about us or the things they may do, but we must know that God will protect us at all costs. Stay focused on God's business, and He will take care of all your concerns—those you are aware of and those you aren't. It's really the best and right thing to do. Don't allow the enemy to get you out of spiritual character; pray about it and leave it in God's hands.

WORD FOR TODAY:

Psalm 31:20 KJV
>[20] Thou shalt hide them in the secret of thy presence from the pride of man: thou shalt keep them secretly in a pavilion from the strife of tongues.

DECEMBER 6

Men and women are real finicky. We are so driven by our emotions. If we are happy, then we will do this or continue to do that, but as soon as we are disgruntled by something, we won't do it. Emotions are fleeting; that's the reason love must be in our hearts. We love God with our whole hearts, and that's why we are driven by our work for God. We must do all things as unto the Lord and not with expectancy from man, knowing God is our rewarder and He will take good care of us.

WORD FOR TODAY:

Colossians 3:23 KJV
>[23] And whatsoever ye do, do it heartily, as to the Lord, and not unto men;

December 7

Thank you for loving me that much, Lord, for we are far greater than the birds and you care for them. I know you care for me. I will not fear man or circumstances. I know you will see me through. I will stand strong.

Word for Today:

Matthew 10:29-31 KJV
> [29] Are not two sparrows sold for a farthing? and one of them shall not fall on the ground without your Father. [30] But the very hairs of your head are all numbered. [31] Fear ye not therefore, ye are of more value than many sparrows.

December 8

God knows, God cares, God can, and God will. Those are my four statements to live by and keep me trusting and believing with my head held high. God is supreme and almighty. He can do what no other can ever do. Live by that truth every day and with every situation that surfaces and watch your victory.

Word for Today:

Philippians 4:19 KJV
> [19] But my God shall supply all your need according to his riches in glory by Christ Jesus.

December 9

I know that God will supply what's sufficient for the day. We waste precious time worrying about this, that, and the other. God doesn't like that. On the contrary, He loves when we put our trust wholly in Him. He is the source of all our supply, and there's nothing He will withhold from us who believe in Him and call on Him with our hearts.

Word for Today:

Psalm 9:10 KJV
> [10] And they that know thy name will put their trust in thee: for thou, Lord, hast not forsaken them that seek thee.

December 10

Regardless of what's going on, who is doing what, and why they are doing it, we must trust God and keep our focus on Him. Know that God would never lead us wrong. Even if it seems a little too much, too steep, or too high, as long as you are following God's lead, you can't fall. You will have a successful end. Though the tide is high, put your focus on God, and it shall not come nigh thee. It's a win-win every time, as long as you are following God's lead. Trust and obey Him and Him only.

Word for Today:

Psalm 23:4 KJV
> [4] Yea, though I walk through the valley of the shadow of death, I will fear no evil: for thou art with me; thy rod and thy staff they comfort me.

December 11

We are in a fleshly body, so it's not strange that we react in the flesh when our emotions starts to overtake us. We have a tendency to react in the natural instead of the spiritual. We speak quickly before we think to seek Holy Spirit's direction. Sometimes silence and no action is the best defense; we fight battles that aren't even ours to fight when all we have to do is stand still and allow God to fight for us. Give God praise through this fight. You won't even feel the impact because God will shield you with His arms of protection. Let go and allow God.

Word for Today:

1 Samuel 17:47 (KJV)
> And all this assembly shall know that the Lord saveth not with sword and spear: for the battle is the Lord's, and he will give you into our hands.

DECEMBER 12

It's so easy to believe what's in front of us, to react to what is seen physically. It takes something extraordinary to look beyond what you see and see as God sees. The Holy Spirit helps us view things in the spiritual, believing God can and will turn things around. He's working it all out for our good. In the natural, naked eye, you are moved by what you see or feel in your emotions. But emotions are fleeting while faith is everlasting. We must condition our minds to believe what God's word says and to walk in it, believing any moment it will come to fruition.

WORD FOR TODAY:

2 Corinthians 5:7 KJV
    [7] (For we walk by faith, not by sight.

DECEMBER 13

It doesn't matter who you are or what your title or economic status may be; you should humble yourself and bow unto our King. Israel's problem was that they were expecting our King to come riding in some fancy, expensive car, with a crown on His head and a robe on His back. God didn't send our Savior in the fashion that they thought He should come, and He wasn't to their liking or satisfaction, so they would not receive Him. But unto us who believe, He gave us power to become the sons of God. Because of Israel's rejection of our Messiah, it brought salvation to us, the Gentiles. The nation of Israel may have refused to bow down, rejecting and crucifying Him, but one day they will bow before our King, as will every man, everywhere.

Word for Today:

Philippians 2:9-10 (KJV)
> Wherefore God also hath highly exalted him, and given him a name which is above every name: [10] That at the name of Jesus every knee should bow, of things in heaven, and things in earth, and things under the earth;

December 14

Word for Today:

1 Peter 1:8-9 (KJV)
> Whom having not seen, ye love; in whom, though now ye see him not, yet believing, ye rejoice with joy unspeakable and full of glory: [9] Receiving the end of your faith, even the salvation of your souls

December 15

Love is your greatest gift to us. You have an everlasting, unconditional love that is hard to comprehend in the natural. As I meditate on my life and on you, I have no excuse for not loving you. You sent your only

Son into this world so that I can live; it's incomprehensible to me. I can't imagine what you or Abraham must have gone through, knowing that you must sacrifice what means most to you in order to save not only me, but the entire universe. I must love like you despite the situation I face, whether good or bad. I must love and live as you did. I know there is nothing I could ever do to change your love for me. Even when I feel that I'm not measuring up to the standard of your holiness, you still love me unconditionally.

My sin, disobedience, and pride separates me from feeling your love, but I know as I love my children, there's nothing I can possibly do to change your agape love for me. I thank you for filling me with your Spirit so that, even though in the flesh I cannot love as you, by your Spirit I can love beyond measure. No matter what is done to me, I can still love unconditionally through your Holy Spirit. Love casts out fear; when I have been perfected in love, I've done according to your commandment. As love is what love does, I won't just say it with my mouth, my actions will also speak love. There is no greater love than this, that a man would lay down his life for his friend. You did just what you said; thus I will do as you would. It's not by my own might neither by my own power, but by your Spirit that I can do all things.

WORD FOR TODAY:

1 John 4:15-18 (KJV)
   Whosoever shall confess that Jesus is the Son of God, God dwelleth in him, and he in God. [16] And we have

known and believed the love that God hath to us. God is love; and he that dwelleth in love dwelleth in God, and God in him. [17] Herein is our love made perfect, that we may have boldness in the day of judgment: because as he is, so are we in this world. [18] There is no fear in love; but perfect love casteth out fear: because fear hath torment. He that feareth is not made perfect in love.

December 16

Rest in knowing that God is our protection; in Him will we go when life seems to be unbearable. God declared when the enemy comes in like a flood that He, Himself, shall lift up a standard against him. We don't always have to fight the battle. When it's too much, hold your head up and look to the hills from which all of our help comes, asking God to intervene. He hears and will step in and win the battle. We won't even feel the effects of the fight because God will place us safely in His arms of protection. He is a mighty fortress; we must lean on His everlasting arms. Hold your peace and let God fight the battle; victory is yours.

Word for Today:

Deuteronomy 33:27 (KJV)
The eternal God is thy refuge, and underneath are the everlasting arms: and he shall thrust out the enemy from before thee; and shall say, Destroy them.

Isaiah 59:19 KJV
> [19] So shall they fear the name of the Lord from the west, and his glory from the rising of the sun. When the enemy shall come in like a flood, the Spirit of the Lord shall lift up a standard against him.

DECEMBER 17

God's mercy endures forever. I don't have to worry or fret. He will work things out for us. Even when the situation looks bleak and we can't see your way through, He steps in and delivers us just before we throw in the towel. We must hang in there; we must know that God is working behind the scenes and will deliver us right on time. He will deliver not just us but all those who are attached to us. He works things out; He wants us to put our trust in His ability. Though things catch us by surprise, nothing catches God by surprise. He is always intentional, and there's something to be learned from the experience. Some lost soul may be saved through this, or our walk with Him will become closer. He is working things in our favor and for +our good.

WORD FOR TODAY:

Psalm 13:5 (KJV)
> But I have trusted in thy mercy; my heart shall rejoice in thy salvation.

December 18

I will live while it is today, staying in your presence all the day long, even while the busy day flows over me. I need that time with you in order to deal with the busy day. It is a luxury that I can't afford to do without. Lord, you know what today will bring, and I don't. Though I may plan and schedule things to complete today, you already know what is before me, and I know you are preparing me for the day. As I stay in your presence, things don't seem to get next to me. I have come to realize that if I could think to give you praise during the most trying times, things would miraculously work out for my good. Nothing catches you by surprise; all things work according to your plan and will work out for my good. All the day, I will be conscious of your abiding presence and seek guidance from you. Though I will do what you have empowered me to do, I will give way for you to do what only you alone can do. I am your workmanship; do with me as you please. I will obey as you speak and allow you to have the preeminence over me. My life is in you alone. Thank you for keeping me in your perfect peace.

Word for Today:

Isaiah 64:4 (KJV)
> For since the beginning of the world men have not heard, nor perceived by the ear, neither hath the eye seen, O God, beside thee, what he hath prepared for him that waiteth for him.

December 19

We should include the Lord in everything that we do and in whatever we set off to do, from morning until night. He already knows what today will bring. He also knows what your plans are and whether you will complete them or not. It's really simple; we make it really hard. There are but twenty-four hours in a day, and there's only so much you can do. Consult the Lord throughout the day on what you should do and what you should let go. When we look to God first, there's nothing He will keep from us. His desire is to supply whatever our needs are, so we must trust Him in all things.

Word for Today:

Proverbs 16:3 KJV
> [3] Commit thy works unto the Lord, and thy thoughts shall be established.

December 20

The one thing we must know is that we are a part of the body of Christ. We are members and members in particular. We all are very significant to God. Who we are matters, what we do matters, and what we say matters because others are watching. There are those among those who are watching—your babies and neighbors alike—some who desire to see you fail and some who want to see you prosper. When we name and claim Jesus as our Savior, we are then under a microscope to those who are in our circle. We are being watched not only for the bad

SCENT OF HEAVEN

but also for the good, so watch your step. Consider the words you speak and make sure you are showing love and kindness in your actions. We must seek and help bring the lost to Christ. God is counting on us.

Word for Today:

John 15:5 (KJV)
> I am the vine, ye are the branches: He that abideth in me, and I in him, the same bringeth forth much fruit: for without me ye can do nothing.

December 21

I was blind, but now I can see clearly in the light of the Lord that our pathway has already been set before us. Walk in that light and help others to see the light of the pathway, so they too may be able to walk therein. As we walk in the light as He is in the light, it will lead us to eternal life in Christ. For in Christ is life and peace; we can bask in Him as freely and as much as we desire and will always be filled. Jesus is a fountain of life, and it flows so that if we drink from the fountain (His word). It cleanses us all of the guilty stains of sin. We grow as we go.

Word for Today:

Psalm 36:9 (KJV)
> For with thee is the fountain of life: in thy light shall we see light

December 22

There is one and only one King of salvation. What king do you know who would sacrifice their life for anyone? It's all about love with our risen King. He is the reason we have life everlasting. He loves us so much in that He suffered, bled, and died just for us — to bring us back to God as incorruptible beings He could present as perfect to God. Nothing anyone else could give would compare to the ultimate Gift Giver. Thank you, Jesus, for your love and for teaching us how to love.

Word for Today:

Matthew 2:9–11 KJV
> [9] When they had heard the king, they departed; and, lo, the star, which they saw in the east, went before them, until it came and stood over where the young child was. [10] When they saw the star, they rejoiced with exceeding great joy. [11] And when they were come into the house, they saw the young child with Mary his mother, and fell down, and worshipped him: and when they had opened their treasures, they presented unto him gifts; gold, and frankincense, and myrrh.

December 23

If I can just get to the house of the Lord, if I can just steal away to my secret closet, if I can just bask in the presence of the Lord, I'll be refreshed and renewed. God is to be honored and reverenced above all else. It is He who has the plan of salvation. He wants us to give Him glory for all that He has done and will do. The holiness of God is beautiful and righteous; we can rest assured as we glorify Him, He gives us the strength we need to go on. We already know that victory is at the end of every challenge we face.

Word for Today:

Psalm 96:6-7 KJV

> [6] Honour and majesty are before him: strength and beauty are in his sanctuary. [7] Give unto the Lord, O ye kindreds of the people, give unto the Lord glory and strength.

December 24

Take a moment today on this eve of the day we recognize as our saviors birthday. While we are shopping and planning to celebrate, Mary the mother of Jesus was challenged to go pay taxes with her fiancé Joseph. While on the way to the city of David (traveling by Camel no doubt), Jesus decided to make His entrance into the world. So as you are challenged with many things on your schedule today, distractions may arise today to throw you off focus or to change whatever plans you have made. Take a few minutes to think about that distraction. It just might be the plan of God that brought that distraction, maybe it will be something that will glorify Him. Perhaps someone needs your help with something, an expected phone call or visitor, maybe even traffic. Whatever the distraction is, be sure to seek God face as to why this distraction that was beyond your control happened. It could be for His glory and not just a distraction to prevent your plans from happening. It's all about Him any way so make sure you glorify Him in all you do today.

WORD FOR TODAY:

Luke 2: 4-6
> [4] And Joseph also went up from Galilee, out of the city of Nazareth, into Judaea, unto the city of David, which is called Bethlehem; (because he was of the house and lineage of David:) [5] To be taxed with Mary his espoused wife, being great with child. [6] And so it was, that, while they were there, the days were accomplished that she should be delivered.

DECEMBER 25

Jesus came through the birth of the Virgin Mary, with no assistance of a man. There's no one who could pay our sin debt; every prophet, priest, and king had tainted blood and could not atone for the sins we committed. God sent His Son in the likeness of sinful flesh to become that pure blood sacrifice. Unselfishly, He gave His life so that we may live and inherit eternal life with the Father. He who knew no sin became sin for us. No greater love than this, that a man would lay his life down for a friend. Jesus said, "I give my life for my friends. You are my friends." Jesus Christ alone can be our sinless Sin-Bearer because only He was born in this miraculous manner.

Word for Today:

Matthew 1:18

> [18] Now the birth of Jesus Christ was as follows: After His mother Mary was betrothed to Joseph, before they came together, she was found with child of the Holy Spirit.

Luke 2:7

> [7] And she brought forth her firstborn son, and wrapped him in swaddling clothes, and laid him in a manger; because there was no room for them in the inn.

December 26

Understand that not everybody who says they are with you and smiles in your face means you well. They could actually be setting you up for your demise. However, God will never allow that to happen. He knows the devices of the enemy and will send a way of escape for you to take. Herod had heard the prophecy of Jesus' birth and was intentionally setting Him up to be killed. God sent the wise men to celebrate His entrance into the world, even though the king sent them to inquire so that he could kill him. We serve a mighty God who knows the intent of the hearts and would not suffer it to be so. People are greedy for money, power, and status and would kill to get it and keep it. We should never be afraid of what the enemy is doing. Know that God has our back and will always keep us from danger,

Word for Today:

Matthew 2:4
> [4] When he had gathered all the chief priests and scribes of the people together, he inquired of them where the Christ was to be born.

December 27

What the enemy meant for evil, God has already worked out for our good. What was meant to be your demise, God turns into your celebration. He will always bring us out on top! It doesn't matter who it is; whether the pope or president of the United States, God will work on your behalf. I'm amazed at how the enemy will stop at nothing to get what's not his; however, I'm encouraged by the fact that just as Jesus withstood Him and fulfilled His destiny, so can we. Don't allow your enemy to paralyze you with fear. God gave us power, love, and a sound mind, so stand on God's word at all times.

Word for Today:

Luke 2:16
> [16}And when they had come into the house, they saw the young Child with Mary His mother, and fell down and worshiped Him.

DECEMBER 28

We cannot change the will of God; it's by divine purpose that we must face our adversaries. If we avoid confrontation, it is just delaying the inevitable. The adversary is a bully. He boasts great threatenings to cause us to fear, and he does it when we are at our weakest moment. He's subtle and cunning; sometimes we don't even see him coming, and before we know it, he overtakes us. We must put on the whole armor of God and keep it on lest at the right moment, he catch us off guard. More times than not, when we are suited with our war garments on, the attack is never to our defeat, but to our victory because we were prepared. Don't let your guard down; saturate yourself with the word of God every day. It's our weapon.

WORD FOR TODAY:

Matthew 4:1
> [1] Jesus was led up by the Spirit into the wilderness to be tempted by the devil. The Holy Spirit led Jesus to a barren place where the devil waited to tempt Him.

DECEMBER 29

Say what you mean and really mean what you say—follow through. Don't make promises that you can't keep. If by chance you don't keep your word, make it right. At least you will not be labeled as a liar. Your word is your bond, so when you give your word, always follow through and know that God honors truth. He declared that a liar will not tarry in His sight. He can't trust anything that the liar says because he starts to believe his own lies. When you say yes, mean yes, and keep your promise; but if the answer is no, say no, and leave it at that.

WORD FOR TODAY:

James 5:12
> [12] Let your "Yes" be "Yes," and your "No," "No." For whatever is more than these is from the evil one.

DECEMBER 30

We have no right to boast about accomplishments that are made. It's only through the power and excellency of God that we are who we are, we do what we do, and live the life we live. It's God who has orchestrated all that pertains to us. Therefore He gets the glory and deserves the praise.

2 Corinthians 4:7 KJV
> [7] But we have this treasure in earthen vessels, that the excellency of the power may be of God, and not of us.

DECEMBER 31

We are of God; it is His peace that keeps us sane in a crazy world. No, the world in its wondrous miraculous existence isn't crazy, but the people are allowing the prince of the power of the air to control their thoughts and actions, resulting in fear, diseases, wars, and hatred. We must trust God always and allow the Holy Spirit to keep our hearts and minds in perfect peace. It is God's will for us to lead long and peaceable lives. Make a choice to live in His peace daily.

Word for Today:

John 14:26-27 KJV

[26] But the Comforter, which is the Holy Ghost, whom the Father will send in my name, he shall teach you all things, and bring all things to your remembrance, whatsoever I have said unto you. [27] Peace I leave with you, my peace I give unto you: not as the world giveth, give I unto you. Let not your heart be troubled, neither let it be afraid.

TAKE AWAYS (NOTES)

CPSIA information can be obtained
at www.ICGtesting.com
Printed in the USA
BVHW071944120719
553339BV00006B/51/P

9 781545 634776